In an intellectual  world dominated by humanistic rationalism, it is good t and demonic reali less. Daniel Juster ness. His approach uncertainties of meaning, and useful for all. Following his analysis of Scripture, Juster brings us into ancient and contemporary witnesses who have encountered spiritual darkness and overcome with the Light of the world.

—DR. DOUG BEACHAM
GENERAL SUPERINTENDENT,
INTERNATIONAL PENTECOSTAL HOLINESS CHURCH

Dan Juster takes us through the Bible on the topic of powers of light and darkness. He sheds a lot of light on the texts, but at the same time he is not trying to answer every possible question. His book is a great guide to study and deepen the understanding of the powers of light and darkness. I am personally impressed with the diligence and depth of Dan's thinking and ability to explain complex issues in a comprehensible way. Thank you, Dan, for your wonderful work.

—MARTIN BUEHLMANN
LEADER OF THE VINEYARD MOVEMENT GERMANY, AUSTRIA,
AND SWITZERLAND AND MEMBER OF THE VINEYARD
EXECUTIVE TEAM

In the 1990s there was some controversy on the subject of spiritual warfare. Some were insistent that the norm in prayer was to directly address demonic principalities and powers to nullify their influence in a particular region. Others taught that this was an aberration, was dangerous, and never should be done. Other issues being discussed at that time were spiritual mapping, identificational repentance, and cleansing the land by breaking curses and removing demon strongholds associated with it. Daniel Juster's book addresses these topics using the Scripture as his foundation for discerning the truth. He gives practical insights on how to go forward on important kingdom activities as we are led by the Spirit leading. This book will help move us forward and into greater unity.

—MIKE BICKLE
INTERNATIONAL HOUSE OF PRAYER OF KANSAS CITY

This clear and comprehensive survey of a difficult subject is essential reading for both students of the Bible and practitioners of healing and help to others.

—JOHN DAWSON,
PRESIDENT EMERITUS, YWAM

Daniel Juster once and for all answers the question, "What does the Bible actually teach us about angels, demons, and spiritual warfare?" This book systematically examines each occurrence of these supernatural beings and uncovers their power for good and evil. If you are looking for a Biblical commentary on what the whole of Scriptures teaches on angels, demons, and spiritual warfare, this is your book.

—DR. JOEY G. WHITE
FOUNDING PASTOR OF STONEWATER CHURCH

There is nothing mystical about "spiritual warfare." The essence of the Great Commission Jesus gives is His directive to advance with the light of the Gospel and the truth of God's Word into the face of a world suffocating in the darkness and smothering within the fog of fumes of hell that seeped and spread across the earth—poisoning the minds and blinding the eyes of humankind.

The light of the world has come in the person of God's Son who is at the same time the way out of the darkness, the truth to shatter error, and the life to resurrect dead humanity wherever any individual will receive Him as the Savior.

Any resource that assists in discerning and resisting vicious activities of Satan's enterprises achieving the adversary's heinous resistance needs to be understood by those who would do battle against the Darkness and advance the Kingdom of Light. This book is a resource to support in that advance and accept those who would be prepared to stand firm for the truth and declare it boldly.

—JACK W. HAYFORD
CHANCELLOR EMERITUS, THE KING'S UNIVERSITY

There's a spiritual battle waging all around us, and we can't ignore it and hope it disappears. It's not going to disappear; and if you don't show up for the fight, you're going to lose. That's why I am grateful for Daniel Juster's important book, *Powers of Light and Darkness*. This book is a valuable tool for those who want to know what the Bible says about spiritual warfare, because knowing the power and truth of God's Word is the only way we're going to win the battle.

—ROBERT MORRIS
FOUNDING SENIOR PASTOR OF GATEWAY CHURCH
AUTHOR OF THE BLESSED LIFE, THE GOD I NEVER KNEW, AND FREQUENCY

POWERS
of LIGHT
and
DARKNESS

DANIEL JUSTER, THD

**CREATION
HOUSE**

Powers of Light and Darkness: Angels, Demons, and Spiritual Warfare by Daniel C. Juster
Published by Creation House
A Charisma Media Company
600 Rinehart Road
Lake Mary, Florida 32746
www.charismamedia.com

Scripture quotations marked KJV are from the King James
Version of the Bible.

Scripture quotations marked BSB are from The Holy Bible,
Berean Study Bible, copyright © 2016 by Bible Hub. Used by
permission. All rights reserved worldwide.

Cover design by Judith McKittrick Wright

Visit the author's website: www.tikkunministries.org

Library of Congress Control Number: 2018906532
International Standard Book Number: 978-1-62999-247-1
E-book International Standard Book Number:
978-1-62999-248-8

While the author has made every effort to provide accurate
telephone numbers and Internet addresses at the time of
publication, neither the publisher nor the author assumes
any responsibility for errors or for changes that occur after
publication.

First edition

18 19 20 21 22—987654321
Printed in the United States of America

CONTENTS

Introduction

THE PLAN OF THIS BOOK

THE PURPOSE OF this book is to provide a brief but comprehensive study about what the Bible says about angels, demons, and spiritual warfare. It is most important that we know just what is found in our texts and what is extrabiblical. The text should always be given more weight than our tradition or the received experiences of believers in Jesus. In some charismatic circles the topic of spiritual warfare is strongly emphasized; and much of the emphasis and teaching is according to the experience of believers in Jesus, their interpretation of their experiences, and sometimes according to one's particular stream of Christian culture. As a Messianic Jew, I do not discredit this but want to be more tied to the texts of the Bible as the foundation. From this foundation we can then weigh what is asserted as taught by experience in dealing with spiritual warfare and deliverance ministries. I will be also providing a selection of quotes separate from the body of the text on the teaching and experiences of many who have been influential in their teaching on this topic.

The Bible gives much less information on this topic than we would conclude from the emphasis and teaching in some charismatic circles. Much of this teaching is based on people's involvement in spiritual warfare prayer, visions, the results of deliverance ministry, and repeated tradition. This does not mean that such teaching is wrong; but again, all of us should first base our understanding on what the Bible says and not assume that the Bible itself is directly teaching what so many are saying. This is a mistake of many who are not biblically educated who presume that such teachings are derived from the Bible. We do want to make sure that nothing taught is contrary to the Bible.

Our plan is to trace the information on this subject mostly according to the Bible's chronological development, partially because we will include the later interpretations within the Bible of the earlier biblical texts.

Another feature of this book is that I have provided quotes from books that I consider classics on spiritual warfare. This is so the reader may gain an understanding of what is presented in the important literature on this subject. We present the material mostly in the order in which it was published. This material is mostly about accounts of spiritual warfare and victory, but we do also use quotes from teaching on spiritual warfare.

lie against me
any false accusation
+ judgment against me
in Jesus name it will come
back to them.

o Lazarus +
Martha

PART I

ANGELS, DEMONS, AND SPIRITUAL WARFARE IN THE HEBREW SCRIPTURES

Chapter 1

THE POWERS OF DARKNESS IN THE TORAH: GENESIS THROUGH DEUTERONOMY

GENESIS 1 THROUGH GENESIS 11

The Garden of Eden

The first appearance in the Bible of an evil and deceptive power is found in Genesis 3. The speaking serpent tempts Eve to make a momentous decision in rebellion to her Creator. Then Adam will follow her lead and also eat of the forbidden fruit of the tree of the knowledge of good and evil. The passage is so familiar to committed Christians and Jews that many miss the strange nature of the passage. Later passages of Scripture connect the spirit behind the serpent as the devil, or Satan. However we do not know this from this passage alone. The figure in the text looks like a talking snake or serpent. Some have wondered about a talking animal. Balaam's donkey also is represented as speaking in Numbers 22. These are the only passages that feature talking animals. In both cases we could question whether it is the animal or a supernatural power working through the animal—for good in Numbers 22 and for evil in Genesis 3. The Bible and the traditions of the Church and synagogue teach that the passage is not about talking snakes but the evil power behind the snake. The passage should be quoted.

> Now the serpent was more cunning than any beast of the field which the LORD God had made. And he said to the woman, "Has God indeed said, 'You shall not eat of every tree of the garden'?" And the woman said to the serpent, "We may eat the fruit of the trees of the garden, but of the fruit of the tree which is in the midst of the garden, God has said, 'You shall not eat if, nor shall you touch it, lest you die.'" Then the serpent said to the women, "You will not surely die. For God knows that in the day you eat of it your eyes will be opened, and you will be like God, knowing good and evil."
>
> —GENESIS 3:1–5, NKJV

The woman later explains her eating by stating that the serpent deceived her (v. 13). The passage on God's response of judgment follows in verses 14–15:

> Because you have done this, You are cursed more than all cattle, And more than every beast of the field; On your belly you shall go, And you shall eat dust All the days of your life. And I will put enmity Between you and the woman, And between your seed and her Seed, He shall bruise your head, And you shall bruise His heel.
>
> —GENESIS 3:14–15, NKJV

These texts are mysterious. First we note that the serpent was more cunning. Now there is no reason to think of a snake in general as particularly intelligent. Serpents do not do a whole lot. Certainly higher mammals would be seen as more intelligent. So the passage cannot only be speaking about snakes. The passage is not speaking about intelligence per se, but cunning, and in this case the ability to deceive through an argument that confused the woman.

There was truth in what the serpent claimed. The eyes of Adam and Eve were opened, and they did have a knowledge of good and evil. In what way? Experientially. They knew the experience of evil, of guilt, shame, and alienation from God. But the truth of the serpent was in part a lie since he claimed that life would be better for them if they ate of the fruit. In addition they could have knowledge by revelation that would enable them to know the good to embrace and the evil to avoid. The serpent's way to know evil is to experience evil by doing evil. So the first evil being portrayed is first known by deceiving.

The curse on the serpent by analogy seems to describe the fact that serpents bite at the heel of people or the lower leg, but people kill a serpent by striking it on the head, bruising it, or crushing it. However, the Bible makes it clear that the being involved is more than a talking snake. The Bible speaks of the seed of the woman killing or bruising the head of the one serpent. It does not speak of bruising the seed of the serpent, but the serpent himself. The enmity is between the seed of the woman and seed of the serpent. Is the seed of the serpent those who give themselves to evil, to other human beings; or does the serpent multiply evil serpent powers? We are not told.

The passage tells us less than we want to know, but later passages look to this one as a key passage speaking of a great evil malevolent power that fosters evil in the world and resists the plans of God. This especially becomes clear in the New Testament Scriptures, but it is the consistent testimony of the rest of the Bible that refers to it. So Adam and Eve are important; they are the vice regents over the creation, called to rule the earth wisely as God's representatives. Therefore the serpent is involved in deceiving the couple that is the apex of God's creation and compromising their rule. We know that serpents do move on the ground and are in the dust at such a level that they would seem to eat dust. The choice of the serpent to be the voice of the devil would thus be a fitting symbol of his real status, a status of being utterly cursed and rejected. Again, natural biology becomes the source of seeing something deeper.

It will be many years in biblical chronology before we have biblical texts explaining the meaning of these passages.

There is one more passage that may be a veiled reference to malevolent power. It is in God's words to Cain in response to Cain's anger over God's rejection of his offering: "If you do well, will you not be accepted? And if you do not do well, sin lies at the door. And its desire is for you, but you should rule over it" (Gen. 4:7, NKJV).

Sin is personified. Is the passage simply being poetic or is it recognizing an evil spiritual power behind sin, a spiritual power that Cain was called to resist and overcome? Of course, he failed and murdered his brother.

The first clear reference to an angel is at the end of Genesis 3:24. We read that "after he drove the man out, he placed on the east side of the Garden of Eden cherubim and a flaming sword flashing back and forth to guard the way to the tree of life."

Cherubim are a type of angel that will make their reappearance in the Torah in representation on the ark and on the tabernacle curtains. The readers or those who received the oral tradition probably knew what these beings were, but our information is very scarce.

The sons of God and the daughters of men
Genesis 6 has generated a great deal of debate. Again, we quote the passage.

Now it came to pass, when men began to multiply
on the face of the earth, and the daughters were
born to them, that the sons of God saw the daughters of men, that they were beautiful; and they took
wives for themselves of all whom they chose. And
the LORD said, "My Spirit shall not strive with man
forever, for he is indeed flesh; yet his days hall be
one hundred and twenty years." There were giants
on the earth in those days, and also afterward, when
the sons of God came into the daughters of men and
bore children to them. Those were the mighty men
who were of old, men of renown. Then the LORD
saw that the wickedness of man was great in the
earth, and that every intent of the thoughts of his
heart was only evil continually.

—GENESIS 6:1–4, NKJV

The text goes on to describe the wickedness of man and
the LORD's decision to destroy mankind. Noah, however,
found grace in the eyes of God and God preserved the
human race through him.

There are two dominant interpretations. The first is
that the daughters of men are the women who are descendants of Cain, whereas the sons of God are the descendants of Seth. God's intent in this interpretation, was to
keep these lines of descent distinct (though the text never
explicitly says this). The language is strange. Weren't the
sons of God also sons of men, descendants of Adam
and Eve? Weren't the daughters of men also the same as
descendants of Adam and Eve? Or is "sons of God" a term
denoting that the descendants of Seth were faithful before
this? Were the other children of Adam and Eve (probably
children were born, at least Seth's wife) also more righteous? At any rate, this is the dominant interpretation

among evangelicals today. The corruption was the intermarriage of a believing line and the unbelieving, thus corrupting the believing line and leading to the corruption of the whole race.

Dissatisfaction with the interpretation above has given rise to a very ancient and popular interpretation. It is that the sons of God were angelic creatures, who either were already fallen or fell in the giving of themselves to women to produce strange offspring described as giants. We find this view in Philo, early rabbinic literature (second to sixth centuries), and also in the early the Church fathers. In this view the term *sons of God* is always used for angels in the Bible except for the King of Israel, who is a son of God. We cannot understand how an angel, who is usually considered a non-sexual being—as is noted in the teaching of Yeshua (Matt. 22:30, NKJV), could change his place and engage with women at such a level that offspring is produced. However, Jude 6-7 seems to indicate the angels left their estate and engaged in sin in parallel to Sodom and Gomorrah later. The term *giants* in Hebrew can also be translated "fallen ones." The corruption of the human race by fallen angels would thus be part of the reason for the flood. The issues of women's head coverings in 1 Corinthians 11 may also be connected to this understanding.

This interpretation is hard for us to fathom. If it is correct, then it gives us some information about fallen angels and may be the first reference to fallen angels and an evil activity in the early period in the Bible. However, we cannot say that this is something that the Bible is clearly saying but something it *may be* saying.

What is the Tower of Babel?

Genesis 11 presents another rebellion. In Genesis 1:28, God commanded Adam and Eve to be fruitful and multiply and fill the earth. Yet we read in Genesis 11:4,

> And they said, "Come, let us build ourselves a city, and a tower whose top is in the heavens; let us make a name for ourselves, lest we be scattered abroad over the face of the whole earth.
>
> —Genesis 11:4, NKJV

There are two dimensions to the rebellion. First, they all desired to stay together in one place and did not plan to fill the earth. God's response was to diversify languages to hasten separation and scattering. This was both a judgment and a blessing. The blessing was in forcing them to fulfill His command. It also prevented unity in rebellion, where they would have greater power to do evil. The multiplication of languages will lead to multiple cultures, which in the Bible is understood as an enrichment of creation (Revelation 22).

The tower is usually understood in connection to false religion. Towers in the ancient world were connected to astrology and the worship of the sun, moon, and stars. We can say that probably Genesis 10 presents a deception of Satan and a false religious direction that connects people to the powers of darkness. So the scattering may be preventing unification under Satanic religion. The text does not clearly say this, but the context of the chapter in the ancient Middle East does have this as a probable implication.

The call of Abram is in a context in which the descendants of Noah were already descending into idolatry and false religion. It appears that Abram's family, the Shemites, were preserving more of the truth from Noah than the rest of the world. I note especially the desire of the patriarchs for their children to marry their cousins. Abram's family appears to be henotheists, those who believed in an ultimate Creator God, but also gave reverence to other gods.

GENESIS 12–50

The rest of the Book of Genesis does give more information. It is clear that a distinction is being made between the family of Abraham and the Canaanites, the former maintaining true faith while the latter is worshipping false gods. We do see Abraham's family maintaining a separation from this corruption. In Genesis 14 we read of the account of Abraham rescuing his family from foreign marauders. After his success in the rescue, we are introduced to the mysterious figure of Melchizedek who is a "priest of God Most High" (Gen. 14:18, NKJV). He meets Abraham upon his return and blesses him. He is a preserver of true faith, and Abraham gives him a tithe. However, Abraham would not take any payment or reward from the King of Sodom. Was this connected in his mind to corruption?

Genesis 18:19–19:29 describes the condition of Sodom and Gomorrah, the utter corruption and perversion. The Bible later connects the level of such sin as connected to evil religious practices, though this is not mentioned in this text. It is thus well to see the situation of Sodom and Gomorrah as connected to dark powers. This is the teaching of Romans 1, that sees idolatry as something that will lead to such corruption.

Genesis 18 and 19 also open us to the concept of angels, otherworldly beings who can materialize and look like human beings. Genesis 18 begins with the statement that "the LORD appeared to Abraham by the *terebinth* trees of

Mamre" (v. 1, NKJV). However verse 2 says that three men appeared to him. As the text progresses we find that one of the three is called the LORD (YWWH—the holy name of God). The other two are just angels. The LORD then dialogues with Abraham about the judgment that He plans. The other two visit Sodom and are mistaken for mere men. The people of the town want to abuse them.

This opens up a great ambiguity concerning the figure of the LORD (YHWH). After this, when the Bible says that an angel appears, it is not clear whether or not it is *the* Angel or the LORD, or another high angelic figure. Some texts make this clear and others do not. In Genesis 18 and 19 it is quite clear. The two angels help Lot escape from Sodom. They also have supernatural powers and are able to blind the people of Sodom to enable Lot and his family to escape. However, the Angel is another figure.

In these texts, we find that angels can take the form of human beings and can appear to men. They are messengers of God with supernatural powers that in all the later texts with angels in the Bible, submitted to God as His messengers. The interaction of angels and also the LORD (YHWH) figure, is found through the rest of the Hebrew Bible.

My view is that when the Bible says, "the Angel of God," or "the Angel of the LORD," we are generally to understand this as the same as YHWH, or the LORD as in Genesis 18. It is evident to me and to many scholars that this figure is the One who is incarnate and became Yeshua the Messiah, deity incarnated into a human being. We see this figure stopping Abraham from slaying Isaac (Genesis 22:11–12), in Genesis 26:24, and in Genesis 28:12–15 where the LORD appears to Jacob in a dream above a ladder where angels are ascending and descending.

In Genesis 31:19 we find that Rachael has stolen the household idols that belonged to her father. These idols would be passed on to the firstborn son as the head of the tribe. The possessor of the idols therefore had rights of inheritance. In the story, Laban catches up to the fleeing Jacob and accuses him of stealing these gods. Rachael avoids being found out by claiming that she is indisposed due to the time of the month. There is some speculation, not found in the text, that this corruption with the gods of Laban opened a door of attack that caused her death. There is as yet no explanation of the powers in idols and a biblical interpretation of idols. However, the idols were understood to carry power from ancestors and gods. Spirits inhabiting idols or being connected to them in some way is the universal consensus of all paganisms, and of course, Rachael was compromised.

In Genesis 32:22–32, we find the very important passage concerning Jacob wrestling with a personage called a man in verse 24. At the end of this well-known story, after Jacob's hip socket was touched leaving him with a limp, we read: "So Jacob called the name of the place Peniel, 'For I have seen God face to face, and my life is preserved'" (v. 30, NKJV).

In Genesis 35:1–4 we read,

> Then God said to Jacob, "Arise, go up to Bethel and dwell there, and make an altar there to God, who appeared to you when you fled from the face of Esau your brother." And Jacob said to his household and to all who were with him, "Put away the foreign gods that are among you, purify yourselves, and change your garments." …So they gave Jacob all the foreign gods which were in their hands, and the earring which were in their ears; and Jacob hid them under the terebinth tree which was by

Shechem. And they journeyed, and the terror of God was upon the cities that were all around them, and they did not pursue the sons of Jacob.

We are not told why Jacob allowed those who were from Laban's house (his servants or maybe even his family) to keep their idols to this point. It is a strange mystery. Yet again, the gods were considered to have supernatural powers, which we now call demonic powers according to later Bible teaching. What is noteworthy is that after they abandoned their gods and dedicated themselves at Bethel, the fear of God came on the surrounding inhabitants. There is here a sense of spiritual warfare in that the protection of God was given by the fear that was tangibly felt by the people of the area. They did not attack Jacob or his contingent.

Joseph in Egypt

There is one significant verse that has implications for spiritual warfare in the Joseph stories. In Genesis 41:8 we are told that the magicians and wise men of Egypt (probably of Pharaoh's court) could not tell Pharaoh the interpretation of his dreams. Was this a power that they commonly had? Did God thwart their interpretive ability? Was this an ability through demonic power? Yes, according to later Christian teaching. However, we are not told in this text. The warfare dimension becomes clear when we realize that Joseph *is* able to do this. In this sense he gains credibility at the expense of the Egyptian magicians and thereby gains governmental authority in Egypt. This prepares the way for his whole family to be saved. The power of God thus defeated the powers of Egyptian magic. The Torah will pick up this again.

11

Exodus

The great contest between Moses and Pharaoh, between the gods of Egypt and the God of Israel, and between the powers of magic and the power of God provides us with the first detailed description of spiritual warfare and the powers of darkness. I think most of our readers know the story. Moses was sent by God to lead the people of Israel to deliverance from Egyptian bondage. There would be a mighty exodus to demonstrate His Lordship to all the nations. To accomplish this task, Moses was given supernatural powers. Signs of this power are described in Exodus, chapter 4. Signs will first convince the people to support Moses.

The contest with Pharaoh begins in chapter 5 with the request of Moses but not until chapter 7 do we see the pitting of supernatural power against supernatural power. In chapter 7, verse 10, Moses and Aaron do their first sign. They cast down Aaron's rod and it becomes a snake. However, Pharaoh's sorcerers and magicians are able to do the same by their enchantments. Their rods become snakes as well. However, here is a big *but*. Aaron's rod swallows up their rods. There is no hint in the text that there was mere trickery on the part of Pharaoh's magicians. It is really a matter of supernatural power against supernatural power.

Pharaoh's hardness of heart leads to the first of the ten plagues. The first is connected to the Nile River. The river turns to blood, whether literal blood or blood in appearance. The fish die and the river stinks. Then the plague is extended to ponds and streams, even pitchers of wood and stone. We read that the magicians with their enchantments are again able to duplicate the miracle. Hence

[handwritten: pharoah + the plagues]

Pharaoh's heart is hardened. Yet we should note that Pharaoh's leaders are not able to remove the plague. This took more power. The text does not note this, but most scholars see this plague and subsequent ones as a battle against the Egyptian gods. In this case, the Nile contained a river god and hence the river god is being defeated. The Nile provided for Egypt's agriculture!

The next plague was a plague of frogs. This probably had reference to the Egyptian frog god, Hopi. Again, the magicians were able to duplicate this. However, only the Lord was able to remove the frogs when Moses and Aaron entreated the Lord. Yet when Pharaoh saw the frogs leave, he again hardened his heart. And so it continues: dust becomes lice, but the magicians cannot duplicate it. They say to Pharaoh, "this is the finger of God" (8:19, NKJV). Next were swarms of flies and a pestilence on livestock, boils on man and beast. In 9:11 we read that the magicians could not stand before Moses because of the boils. Again we see the superiority of the God of Israel.

In 9:16 we read these words spoken to Pharaoh, "For this purpose I have raised you up. that I may show My power in you, and that My name may be declared in all the earth." A plague of hail follows this, and those who did not fear God lost their livestock. *[handwritten: Pray that your enemy would fear God OR judgment will come]*

In these plagues God made a distinction between the Egyptian living areas and the territory where Israel dwelled. Israel was plague free.

In chapter 10 the plague of locust is announced and then a plague of darkness. This plague of darkness struck at the heart of Egypt's religion, namely the worship of the sun as their chief god. Then finally the last plague was the death of the firstborn over the land of Egypt. Again, this has implications for spiritual warfare, since in Egyptian

[handwritten: Also did not fear God: Math 18: 27-30 — His master forgave Him his debt - of money owed. yet he put in prison the man who owe him]

religion the Pharaoh and his firstborn son were an incarnation of the sun god, *Re*. Finally Pharaoh, Egypt, and their gods were defeated, or almost finally defeated. There was still one more battle, and that is the exodus through the sea and the drowning of Pharaoh's pursuing troops.

The Exodus is the beginning of a constant biblical theme. Israel is, throughout her history, in a battle against the gods of the other nations. Here she is victorious against the most powerful nation known in that region of the world, and to their knowledge perhaps the whole world. The victory proves that the God of Israel is more powerful than the gods of Egypt and is the Lord over all the earth. In the ancient mind, the one who is victorious in war has superior and more powerful gods. The conquered nation submits to the conqueror, but the gods also become subservient. Thus the battles between Israel and the nations in the land of Canaan, and against the surrounding nations, are battles against the gods of those nations. The battles are supernatural. The theme that begins in the Exodus carries through the Hebrew Bible. Sometimes that battle is within due to Israel's compromise in idolatry with the nations around them, but sometimes it is a battle in war against those without. The gods of the nations are inferior. How were the gods defeated? By the anointing of power on those who led Israel in the battle through prayer and obedience.

The Bible states that the physical idols are nothing. They cannot hear or see. This is a constant refrain. Yet the Bible also shows that behind the idols are gods with power. The power is limited and totally inferior to the God of Israel. They are defeated in a context of submission to God, prayer, and worship. It is not until the later Old Testament texts and the New Testament, as reflected in the literature that

14

was written between the Old and New Testaments, that we see the gods described as great demonic powers over nations and earthly territories.

The rest of Exodus and Leviticus give important information on the Law of God. There is no information on contests or war between God and the gods, but there are important commands against practices that connect people to false gods and, from a New Testament perspective, demonic powers. For example, Exodus 22:20: "He who sacrifices to any god, except to the LORD only, he shall be utterly destroyed." Also in Exodus 23:13: "Make no mention of the name of other gods, nor let it be heard from your mouth." Then in chapter 22, verse 18: "You shall not permit a sorceress to live." Israel must not practice any divination. These strict standards call Israel to purity so that she can be a light to the nations. There must be no compromise with the powers of the gods or the dark forces of witchcraft. Deuteronomy will repeat these prohibitions.

The Exodus artwork and its implications

There is a paradox at the heart of the Torah. The Covenant of the Ten Words (Ten Commandments) tells us that we are not to make any image of either God or of heavenly creatures or of earthly creatures. This is directly after the command to have no other gods. Two passages are surprising in the light of this prohibition. They are the exceptions to the rule and were commanded by God.

The first is the creation of the two cherubim:

> Then he made two cherubim out of hammered gold at the ends of the cover. He made one cherub on one end and the second cherub on the other; at the two ends he made them of one piece with the cover. The cherubim had their wings spread upward,

overshadowing the cover with them. The cherubim
faced each other, looking toward the cover.

—Exodus 37:7–9

Bible scholars generally agree that the cherubim represent high angels that serve in the presence of God.
Hebrews did not invent the idea that the tabernacle was a
copy of heavenly realities.

Also we read of the interior curtain, "They made the
curtain of blue, purple and scarlet yarn and finely twisted
linen, with cherubim woven into it by a skilled worker"
(Exod. 36:35).

The meaning of these figures bespeaks the transcen-
dence and majesty of God, but in Ezekiel we find that such
figures are more than symbolic. Powerful angels serve in
the very most intense place of the presence of God.

Numbers

The Book of Numbers, however, presents us with an
important window into spiritual warfare and the powers
of darkness in chapter 22. This is the story of Balak,
the king of Moab, and of Balaam who appears to be a
prophet. The story is very familiar, especially the account
of Balaam's donkey, who was hindered by an angel from
continuing on the road. Of course, we remember that
Balaam's donkey spoke, whether himself or by an angel
speaking through him.

The King of Moab desired that Balaam would come
with his men and from the heights of Moab and would
curse the Israelites. (So the implication is that the king
knew that there was spiritual power in a prophetic person
who spoke a curse more than he the king could affect.) It
appears that Balaam knew something of God, could seek

God, and could gain words from Him (Num. 22:8). God at first commanded Balaam not to go with them and he did not go. Yet when the king sent more nobles and Balaam again sought a word from God, he was given permission to go. God said that he was only to speak what God would tell him to speak. So Balaam did go, but something changed. Did Balaam intend to disobey God for riches or honor? We are not told, but the Angel of the LORD appeared and blocked the way. Again the Angel said that he could go but again to only speak what He commanded.

In chapter 23 we read that Balaam received the word from God, and instead of cursing Israel he spoke wonderful blessings over them in wonderful Hebrew verse. Good English versions capture the poetry. He sought the LORD three times and came out with wonderful blessings. In 23:23 he delivers this word, "For there is no sorcery against Jacob, Nor any divination against Israel." Balak in great anger commanded Balaam to flee to his place. More accurate prophecy is delivered, including a Messianic prophecy.

However, the story does not end here. In chapter 25, the Israelites committed "harlotry with the women of Moab" (v. 1, NKJV). Judgment was now upon Israel, but Phineas turned back God's wrath by exacting judgment on an Israelite who was blatantly, brazenly public in his sin. He killed the man and the woman, and the plague was stopped, but not before twenty-four thousand perished. Only later in the Torah do we find that Balaam was behind the harlotry that took place, and no doubt this harlotry was religious in nature and included involvement with the false gods of Moab.

Chapter 31 recounts Israel taking revenge on the Midianites for the incident of harlotry. In both chapter

17

25 and chapter 31 we see that Midianites and Moabites were involved together. Chapter 31:16 states that these women "caused the children of Israel, through the counsel of Balaam, to trespass against the Lord." Balaam must have known that if Israel committed harlotry with these women and idolatry, they would lose God's protection and could be defeated by their enemies. It is amazing that he would do this after the prophecies he delivered. Balaam remains an enigmatic figure. But the lesson on warfare is that God's people can be defeated by yielding to temptation. The specific temptation that yielded to evil power in this case was through an idolatry with religious harlotry.

DEUTERONOMY

In Deuteronomy we find the most important passage in the Torah that forbids involvement in false spiritual participation. We quote it in full.

> When you come into the land which the LORD your God is giving you, you shall not learn to follow the abominations of those nations. There shall not be found among you anyone who makes his son or his daughter pass through the fire, or one who practices witchcraft, or a soothsayer, or one who interprets omens, or a sorcerer, or one who conjures spells, or medium, or a spiritist, or one who calls up the dead. For all who do these things are an abomination to the LORD, and because of these abominations to the LORD your God drives them out from before you. You shall be blameless before the LORD your God. For these nations which you dispossess listened to soothsayers and diviners; but as for you, the LORD your God has not appointed such for you.
>
> —DEUTERONOMY 18:9–14, NKJV

Contrary to this false spirituality, which is forbidden, God promises to raise up prophets. They can guide Israel into her future, and indeed there will be one great prophet who will be like Moses in all regards.

There is nothing in the passage that denies that there is something of real power in these pagan practices. However, these practices are abhorrent to God, and not just unlawful for Israel. These practices are the reason why God is driving them out of the land. I believe that this passage is a key to the mystery of why Israel had to destroy the Canaanites. It was like Sodom and Gomorrah throughout the land. Indeed, when people are so given to the powers of darkness and gross immorality, connection to the occult passes to their children. There was no deliverance ministry in the name of Yeshua at that time. The children of these people would have grown up with occult powers and demonic possession. So only eliminating them would enable Israel to be a light to the surrounding nations.

Just what are people connecting to when they engage in these practices? How do we describe the realm of darkness? We have to await further light from other biblical writings. We already at this point see that power can be exercised from the realm of darkness as well as from a realm of light.

EXCURSUS

Jesse Penn-Lewis, *War on the Saints*

This classic has some controversial teachings on what is deception and what is really from God that is still debated today. It should be read without assuming all its points of view are true. Yet the book has much value. Here is an excerpt:

The commission he gave to the twelve, and to the seventy was exactly in line with His own. He sent them forth, and "gave them authority over unclean spirits, to cast them out and to preach the gospel." (Mt. 10:1); to "first bind the strong man" (Mk. 3:27; top), and then to take his goods: to deal with the invisible hosts of Satan first, and then "preach the gospel."

From all this we learn that there is one Satan, one devil, one prince of the demons, directing all the opposition to Christ and His people; but myriads of wicked spirits called "demons," lying spirits, deceiving spirits, foul spirits, unclean spirits, subjectively at work in men. Who they are, and whence their origins, none can positively say. That they are spirit beings who are evil is alone beyond all doubt; and all who are undeceived and dispossessed from Satanic deception, become witnesses, from their own experience, to their existence, and power....From experience they know that they are hindered by spirit beings, and therefore know that these things are done by evil spirits who are hinderers. Therefore, reasoning from experimental facts, as well as the testimony of Scripture, they know that these evil spirits are murderers, tempters, liars, accusers, counterfeiters, enemies, haters, and wicked beyond all the power of man to know.

Excerpt taken from *War on the Saints* by Jessie Penn-Lewis. Used by permission of CLC Publications. May not be further reproduced. All rights reserved.

Watchman Nee, *Sit, Walk, Stand*

This famous Christian leader provided us with a classic story of a power encounter with the powers of darkness.

This is a shortened account that took place on a Chinese Island.

The New Year holiday is a long one, lasting fifteen days....It is also the best time for Gospel preaching...so I planned to take with me five brothers for a fifteen-day preaching visit to an island off the South China coast....Though we found the people of the village most courteous, we had very little fruit from the island, and we began to wonder why this was.

On January 9th we were outside preaching. Brother Wu with some others was in one part of the village and suddenly asked publicly: "Why will none of you believe?" Someone in the crowd replied at once: "We have a god—one god—Ta-wang, and he has never failed us. He is an effective god." "How can you know that you can trust him?" asked Wu. "We have held his festival procession every January for 286 years. The chosen day is revealed by divination beforehand, and every year without fail his Day is a perfect one without rain or cloud," was the reply. "When is the procession this year?" "It is fixed for January 11th at eight in the morning." "Then," said brother Wu impetuously, "I promise you that it will certainly rain on the 11th." At once there was an outburst of cries from the crowed: "That is enough! We don't want to hear any more preaching. If there is rain on the 11th, then your God is God."

I was elsewhere in the village when this occurred. As soon as I heard of it, I saw that it was most serious....We stopped our preaching at once and gave ourselves to prayer.... Had we made a terrible mistake, or dare we ask God for a miracle? ...Then, like a flash, there came the word to me: "Where is the God of Elijah?" It came with such clarity and power that I knew it was from God. Confidently I announced to the brothers: "I have the answer. The Lord will send rain on the eleventh." Together we thanked Him, and then full of praise, we went out—all seven of us—and told everyone....If you prefer a rationalistic explanation [re: Ta-Wang and the weather] here was a whole village of fisherman.... They, of all people, should know by long experience when it would not rain for two or three days ahead.

This disturbed us....We all began once more to pray for rain—*now!* Then it was that there came to us a stern rebuke from the Lord: "Where is the God of Elijah?" ...

I was awakened by the direct rays of the sun through the single window of our attic. "This isn't rain!" I said. It was already past seven o'clock.... "Lord," I said, "please send the rain!" But once again ringing in my ears came the word: "Where is the God of Elijah?" ...We sat down to breakfast—eight of us together, including our host—all very quiet. There was no cloud in the sky, but we knew God was committed. As we bowed to say grace before the food I said, "I think the time is up. Rain must come now. We can bring it to the Lord's remembrance." Quietly we did, and this time the answer came with no hint whatsoever of rebuke in it.

"*Where is the God of Elijah?*" Even before our "Amen" we heard a few drops on the tiles. There was a steady shower as we ate our rice and were served with a second bowl. "Let us give thanks again," I said, and now we asked God for heavier rain. As we began on that second bowl of rice, the rain was coming down in bucketfuls. By the time we had finished, the street outside was already deep in water, and the three steps at the door of the house were covered.

Soon we heard what had happened in the village. Already, at the first drop of rain, a few of the younger generation had begun to say openly: "There is God; there is no more Ta-wang! He is kept in by the rain." But he wasn't. They carried him out on a sedan chair. Surely he would stop the shower! Then came the downpour. After only some ten or twelve yards, three of the coolies stumbled and fell. Down went the chair and Ta-wang with it, fracturing his jaw and his left arm. Still determined, they carried out emergency repairs and put him back in the chair. Somehow, slipping and stumbling, they dragged or carried him halfway round the village. Then the floods defeated them. Some of the village elders, old men of 60 to 80 years, bareheaded and without umbrellas as their faith in Ta-wang's weather required, had fallen and were in serious difficulties. The procession was stopped, and the idol taken into a house. Divination was made. "Today was the wrong day," came the answer. "The festival is to be on the fourteenth with the procession at six in the evening."

Immediately we heard this there came the assurance in our hearts: "God will send rain on the fourteenth at 6:00 P.M. and give us four good days until then." That afternoon the sky cleared and now we had a good hearing for the Gospel. The Lord gave us over thirty converts—real ones—in the village and in the island during those three short days. The fourteenth broke, another perfect day, and we had good meetings. As the evening approached, we met; and again, at the appointed hour, we quietly brought the matter to the Lord's remembrance. Not a minute late, His answer came with torrential rain and floods as before....

For us the essential point was that Satan's power in that idol had been broken, and that is an eternal thing.

Excerpts taken from *Sit, Walk, Stand* by Watchman Nee, copyright © 1957 by Angus I. Kinnear. Used by permission of CLC Publications. May not be further reproduced. All rights reserved.

Chapter 2

SPIRITUAL WARFARE IN JOB AND THE HISTORICAL BOOKS: JOSHUA THROUGH 2 SAMUEL

THE BOOK OF JOB

THE BOOK OF Job presents us with many unsolved and perhaps unsolvable questions. Many conservative scholars believe that the book was written before the time of the Patriarchs. It seems to predate the knowledge of the Abrahamic and Mosaic Covenants and reflects the life a faithful person just prior to that time. The cultural context seems very parallel to the patriarchal period. More liberal scholars think the book is a later creation since they see the ideas about God as more in keeping with the later period of Israel's history.

The book presents us with the strange picture of Satan going before God and challenging God's evaluation of Job as a righteous and faithful man. The name Satan means accuser, and he is certainly accusing Job and for no good reason. That Satan can come into the presence of God in the way described in Job is puzzling. Some believe this is a literary device and Satan, though challenging Job with God's permission, did not literally come before God in this way. Others believe there was a time that Satan had access to God—though an evil and fallen archangel—but that after the death and resurrection of Yeshua, he was cast down and lost this access. I do not think it is important to settle these questions to get an understanding of the important teaching of Job for the purposes of this book.

In addition, we find ourselves puzzled as to just what happened. Is it really possible that Job sat in agony with his friends and with them produced the amazing quality of narrative poetry that is recorded in the Book of Job? Who was the secretary taking down these amazing artistic pieces and how were they so well composed in the setting? As soon as we ask these questions we realize that the author of Job presents a highly polished piece of literature representing the great trial of Job after the events with the response of his friends.

Let us summarize the book briefly and then apply it to our topic. The representation of Job as a righteous man is not to be doubted or explained away as if some level of sin and doubt was the cause of his own problems. If this was so, the speeches of his friends would have been correct; but they were severely rebuked by God as missing the mark.

Job is described in 1:1 NKJV, as "blameless and upright, and one who feared God and shunned evil." He was a man blessed with great possessions with many sons, daughters, and servants. He offered burnt offerings to God and also sought to intercede by sacrifices for his sons.

In 1:6 the sons of God (no doubt angels) come before God and Satan is among them. This seems very strange to us. God brags about Job to Satan that "there is no one on earth like him; he is blameless and upright, a man who fears God and shuns evil" (v. 8).

What is Satan's accusation? That Job only lives as he does because of God's protection and blessing, that his commitment is not to God for Himself—for if he loses what he has, Satan predicts that he will curse God.

This leads to a succession of trials where Job loses his livestock, his servants, and finally his sons and daughters. Job's response is submission to God, "The LORD gave and the LORD has taken away; Blessed be the name of the LORD" (v. 21, NKJV). He did not charge God with wrong.

Going to chapter 2, we find God again asserting that Job has his integrity and shuns evil though Satan incited God against him (v. 3). Then finally God allows Satan to bring a torturous disease or diseases upon Job so that even his wife says, "Curse God and die!" (v. 9). Job responds, "Shall we accept good from God, and not trouble?" The text concludes, "In all this, Job did not sin in what he said" (v. 10).

Job's friends sit in stunned silence for seven days and seven nights. That was the right response. However, the following chapters until chapter 32 generally show Job's friends responding by arguing that Job must have done something wrong to bring this judgment and that he needed to repent. Neither the friends nor Job know that the issue was not a matter of Job's specific sin but God allowing a test to prove Job's loyalty and commitment to God. So chapter after chapter provides us with general truth concerning sowing and reaping. The chapters are full of much wisdom and are generally true, *but!* Any word of faith type teacher (Tulsa theology) would find his theology well represented in these chapters, but this theology does not apply to Job. Job denies the accusations of his friends and asserts his innocence. He does cry out concerning his seemingly unfair treatment and cries for a chance to come before God to make his case.

In chapter 32 the speeches of Elihu bring us closer to the truth that the author of Job is seeking to convey. It is that we are finite, and God is way beyond us and we cannot call His ways into question. All that God does is right even if it does not so appear. For God never does what is wicked, but He is so sovereign that we best not call Him into question. However, Elihu still does not transcend the idea that Job must have done something wrong, but he sees him as wrong to so severely question God.

Finally, God reveals Himself to Job in His awesome majesty. Job is speechless. Job, having seen God, (42:6) states, "I despise myself and repent in dust and ashes."

After all this, God says that Job's friends are basically in the wrong, "because you have not spoken the truth about me, as my servant Job has" (v. 7). They therefore are to take seven bulls and seven rams and go to Job with them as a burnt offering and Job is to pray for them. Job's intercession prevents their judgment.

Finally God restored Job's fortunes, twice as much as before. His brothers, sisters, and acquaintances came before him and consoled him. Job also had seven sons and three daughters. After this Job lived one hundred and forty years.

Let us not try to solve the mysteries that we outlined at the beginning of this section. Rather, let us take from the book that which is consistent with the rest of Scripture.

First, the Book of Job presents a figure called Satan who is an accuser of Job. This fits the later Bible picture of the devil or Satan as the accuser of the brethren (Rev. 12:10). Second, Satan can do nothing, especially to a righteous person, without God's permission. Satan may test but he does not have the power to destroy the righteous.

Third, Job unknowingly overcomes Satan by refusing to fall into the temptation to curse God and give up his integrity. Integrity is here defined as loyalty to God. This is on the basis of who God is. There is no direct prayer against the devil, no commands against him, and no taking authority over the attack. Job overcomes by merely going through the trial in a basically faithful way, though with plenty of complaints in the suffering. He is finally both corrected and exonerated. The Bible will give us more information on how to overcome the devil and how to resist him, but at this point we do see some basic information that will be consistently affirmed in the Bible.

THE HISTORICAL BOOKS (PRE-EXILIC IN CONTENT)

We will look at the references in the historical books as one section of writings—Joshua through 2 Chronicles—though we should recognize 2 Chronicles as much later. We will find that the realm of darkness is connected to occult practices and idolatry. The historical books thus reflect the passage in Deuteronomy that forbade these practices.

The Book of Joshua

The first significant reference is in Joshua 5:13. Joshua looks and sees a Man standing opposite him with His sword drawn in His hand. He goes up to Him and asks, "Are You for us or for our adversaries?" His answer is, "No, but as Commander of the army of the LORD I have now come" (v. 14, NKJV). Then we read,

> And Joshua fell on his face to the earth and worshipped, and said to Him, "What does my Lord say to His servant?" Then the Commander of the LORD's army said to Joshua, "Take your sandal off your foot, for the place where you sand is holy." And Joshua did so.
>
> —JOSHUA 5:14–15, NKJV

Are we reading of the same figure in chapter 6:2, when we read, "And the LORD said to Joshua, 'See! I have given Jericho into your hand…'"?

Thus we have ambiguity. We will later read of very high angels such as Michael and Gabriel. Michael is a leading warrior angel, so could this be the figure we later see as Michael? Or is the figure in 6:2 who speaks the same as the one in 5:14. In that verse Joshua does not address Him as LORD, or YHWH, but only as Adoni, the common word for Lord and not God. Yet the taking off of the shoes and holy ground is reminiscent of the Angel of the LORD figure in Exodus 3 that is also addressed as LORD or YHWH, the holy name of God.

It is interesting to note that there is a Christian interpretive tradition that is repeated over and over though there is no basis in the text. When the figure that appears to Joshua concerning his question of whose side the man is on, he answers, "No." So commonly preachers say he was saying I am not on your side or their side. But this is obviously wrong since the Angel figure is on the side of Joshua and He will be empowered to conquer Jericho. The no is in answer to the misunderstanding that he is a man. It is, "No, I am not a man as you are thinking." Rather He is the commander of the LORD's army. And what is this army? Here we find the first verses that probably indicate an army of angels or heavenly beings. The Angel is not saying that He is the commander of the armies of Israel. We could read it this way, but we will read in the later historical books of the unseen angelic army of God.

The other key aspect in Joshua is the command to totally destroy the Canaanites. Here we read the description of the task in 6:17, NKJV: "The city shall be doomed by the Lord to destruction, it and all who are in it. Only

Rahab the harlot shall live, she and all who are with her in the house, because she hid the messengers that we sent."

It is popular among some who even claim to be Evangelicals that God never gave Joshua such a command. But this command is affirmed as having been given again and again throughout the Hebrew Bible. It is in a context of God being merciful and waiting over 400 years until the iniquity of the Amorite was full. (See Genesis 15:16.) This is made most clear in Judges when the Angel of the LORD appears and speaks, certainly YHWH in manifestation. Judges 2:1–4 (NKJV) states,   *Yahweh = the God of Israel*

> Then the Angel of the LORD came up from Gilgal to Bochim, and said, "I led you up from Egypt and brought you to the land of which I swore to your fathers; and I said, 'I will never break My covenant with you. And you shall make no covenant with the inhabitants of this land, you shall tear down their altars.' But you have not obeyed My voice. Why have you done this? Therefore I also said, 'I will not drive them out before you, but they shall be thorns in your side, and their gods shall be a snare to you.'"
> So it was, when the Angel of the LORD spoke these words to all the children of Israel that the people lifted up their voices and wept.

Judgment when they did the Israeli did obey not God.

I put forth a reasonable speculation. The powers of the false gods were occult powers. The false religions of Canaan could draw the people away from God. However, in addition, when a culture is thoroughly given over to sin and the occult, the demonic powers are inherited by the children. There was no power for deliverance in the name of Yeshua to cast out the demons. Israel could only be a light to the nations around them by eliminating the

no elimination

wicked and totally demonized Canaanites who were similar to Sodom and Gomorrah throughout the land. The wickedness was exceedingly wicked and required the elimination of the whole culture and the whole people of the land. No other explanation can provide a rational for this difficult command of genocide.

The Book of Judges

We need not present all the passages in the Book of Judges that speak of spiritual warfare. They are all of a similar nature. Generally, Israel does evil. That evil is usually described as falling into idolatry or occult practices. This is through the influence of the people that Israel did not destroy. In Judges the word of the prophet states, "I said to you, 'I am the LORD your God; do not worship the gods of the Amorites, in whose land you live.' But you have not listened to me" (6:10). From now on we can interpret the historical books as the battle between the God of Israel and the false gods of the nations—a battle between light and darkness and, we would say now, the godly realm and the demonic realm. The battle began in Egypt, but from now on the issue is compromise.

In the account of the calling of Gideon, we read about the compromise in his own family, for the LORD says to Gideon,

> Tear down your father's altar to Baal and cut down the Asherah pole beside it. Then build a proper kind of altar to the LORD your God on the top of this height. Using the wood of the Asherah pole that you cut down, offer the second bull as a burnt offering.
> —JUDGES 6:25–26

So compromised were the men of the town that they say to his father, "Bring out your son, He must die, because he has broken down Baal's altar and cut down the Asherah pole beside it" (v. 30). Gideon's father responds, "If Baal really is a god, he can defend himself when someone breaks down his altar" (v. 31). The idea of a great contest between the true and false is now a continual theme.

Gideon wins the battles of the LORD through His supernatural help. Israel is delivered from oppression. And yet after all this, Gideon made an ephod. This is a probably a type of lot for divining the will of God, but Israel treated it wrongly and prostituted themselves by worshipping it. It was so very difficult to keep Israel from the occult and from false worship. Yet they kept free from Baal worship and there was peace for forty years. After Gideon's death, however, the people returned to Baal worship. They also forgot to be kind to the family of Gideon. (See Judges 8.)

Again, during the days of Jephthah, Israel turned to other gods and then was oppressed by the other nations. When Israel finally cried out to the LORD, He responded,

> When the Egyptians, the Amorites, the Ammonites, the Philistines, the Sidonians, the Amalekites, and the Maonites oppressed you and you cried to me for help, did I not save you from their hands? But you have forsaken me and served other gods, so I will no longer save you. Go and cry out to the gods you have chosen. Let them save you when you are in trouble.
>
> —JUDGES 10:11–12

Israel responded to this rebuke by getting rid of the foreign gods and serving the LORD, who we read could not bear Israel's misery and sent Jephthah. Again we find deliverance of Israel through supernatural help.

Samson

The birth story of Samson again presents us with the Angel of the LORD figure who appears to be part of the identity of God. The Angel promises a son to Manoah and his wife. It appears that his father Manoah thinks this Angel is a man—a human prophet. But when the Angel ascended on the flame of the sacrifice requested by the Angel, Manoah realized that it was the Angel of the LORD and says, "We shall surely die because we have seen God!" (13:22, NKJV). But she says, "If the LORD [YHWH] had desired to kill us, He would not have accepted a burnt offering and grain offering from our hands, nor would He have told us such things as these at this time" (v. 23, NKJV).

Compromise

Chapters 17 and 18 of the Book of Judges are pivotal chapters in the prophetic interpretation of the nation of Israel. The issues of compromise with paganism continues with the story of Micah in chapter 17, who lives in the hill country of Ephraim. In this story Micah makes a carved image made from silver which he consecrates to the LORD. The LORD is still the object of worship, but now through a forbidden image. He further makes a shrine, an ephod, and some idols, and he installs one of his sons as a priest. However, knowing of the status of the Levitical priesthood, he later installs a Levite from Judah. Theologians call the theology of Micah, henotheism. There is one ultimate God but other gods as well. For Micah, that ultimate God is YAHWEH.

Chapter 18 tells the story of how the Danites who were not able to conquer their allotted inheritance went through Ephraim. A scouting team inquired of the Levite (probably through the ephod). After their scouting journey they met with the rest of the men going forth to conquer territory for their inheritance. They decided to steal the ephod, the household gods, the carved image, and the idol (probably a representation of YHWH, which was forbidden) and to take the Levite to be their priest. They then conquered Laish in the north and renamed it Dan. There they set up the idols. This set a precedent for the northern tribes of Israel. Later, King Jeroboam would follow this precedent in setting up his bull images as the images for worshipping in the North and thereby breaking from the Jerusalem worship center.

Spiritual warfare is thus a battle within Israel. Sometimes Israel compromises to the gross level of worshipping Baal and his consort Asherah. Sometimes they compromise by making an idol to represent the LORD. Sometimes they fall into henotheism, with one ultimate God but also recognizing lesser gods.

The Book of 1 Samuel

Finally, God raises up a mighty prophet judge, Samuel, to deliver Israel and to turn them back from compromise. *good time for Israel* The battle against the false gods theme continues in the Book of 1 Samuel. A most noteworthy story appears from chapters 5 and 6. The priesthood had become corrupt under the leadership of the sons of Eli, the high priest. The nation was in need of repentance and restoration. In this state the Israelites lost a major war with the Philistines and the ark of the Covenant was captured. Eli's corrupt sons, Hophni and Phinehas, were slain. Eli died upon hearing the news. (See 1 Samuel 4: 10–18.)

The presence and power of God or "the glory" was connected to the ark. The people of Ashdod put the ark in their temple before their god Dagon. It was a normal practice to join gods together under the god whose people had won the war. But the ark was not a god; it was the place of the presence of God and the box where His covenant tablets were kept.

We read in chapter 5 that during the night, the Philistine god Dagon fell on his face on the ground before the ark. The second morning revealed a more serious happening. The god had fallen on the ground and his head and hands were broken. In addition to this, the people were afflicted with tumors. They rightly interpreted the situation, namely that the God of Israel was against them. They first moved the ark to Gath, but the people panicked when tumors broke out upon them. So they sent the ark to Ekron, but the people would not receive it. The people of Ekron called on the rulers to send the ark back to Israel. Some died, and others were afflicted with tumors.

Chapter 6 tells us that the Philistines then called upon the priests and diviners to know what they should do. They were advised to send the ark back to Israel with a guilt offering. What was this guilt offering to be? It was to be five gold rats and five models of the tumors, both according to the number of the Philistine rulers. By this they were to pay homage to the God of Israel. This leads me to believe that the plague of judgment was a bubonic plague which is a sickness connected to rat fleas and to tumors. They place the ark on a cart to be pulled by two cows that have never been yoked.

In verse 9 the priests and diviners put forth the idea that if the ark goes toward Beth Shemesh, the LORD brought the disaster, but if it does not, then it was not of His hand but happened by chance. This ability to know that some things happen by the power of the gods and some things by the normal course of events shows significant understanding. Of course, the cart goes to Beth Shemesh. The whole incident demonstrates the superiority of God over all other gods. The people of Beth Shemesh offered the cows as a sacrifice and the wood of the cart to burn the offering.

Such power was connected to the ark that seventy men were struck down because they looked into the ark and violated the priestly rules for the ark. This resulted in such a level of fear that the people decided to send the ark away to the men of Kiriath Jearim. They brought it to the house of Abinadab and consecrated Eleazar his son to guard the ark (7:1).

This incident gives some indication of spiritual warfare and the important understanding that the powers of the gods of the nations are greatly inferior to the God of Israel. Israel's defeat is due to sin and compromise, never due to God being less powerful. Therefore winning spiritual battles requires that God's people be wholly committed to Him and His ways.

Chapter 7:2–17 describes a good period for Israel under the leadership of the prophet judge Samuel. The Israelites mourned after the LORD and Samuel called them to rid themselves of all foreign gods to serve God only. From this time on, the Philistines were defeated by Israel with supernatural power. The battle against the Philistines was not merely a human battle or to be understood according to that which is visible but was a spiritual warfare. The LORD threw them into a panic. There were about twenty years of peace.

Amazingly in chapter 8 we find that when Samuel grew, he appointed his sons as judges, but they were corrupt and accepted bribes and perverted justice. The deterioration under these sons prompted Israel to ask for a king. The issue of a king for Israel is very interesting, but not immediately germane to our subject. The rest of the Book of

[handwritten marginal notes: "After they repent", "70 yrs peace"]

1 Samuel tells us the story of Saul's kingship and the personage of David who served in his court until fleeing for his life. It should be noted that the defeat of Goliath at the hand of David had that mark of supernatural power and would have been understood as a defeat of the Philistine gods once more.

There is an important indication of the power of evil spirits in the account of Saul's jealousy of David. We read in 1 Samuel 16:14, "Now the Spirit of the LORD had departed from Saul and an evil spirit from the LORD tormented him." Saul's attendants recognize this evil spirit and seek someone to play the harp so he can overcome the manifestation of the evil spirit (whether it was in depression, sickness, or other we are not told, only that it tormented him). When David played, the evil spirit would leave. How and why this worked is never explained. In 1 Samuel 18:10-11, under the influence of an evil spirit from God, Saul hurled a spear at David to pin him to the wall. It is interesting that in these instances the evil spirit is under God's control, David is protected from Saul's behavior, and the evil spirit serves God's purpose and leads to David's fleeing the house of Saul.

We end our discussion of the Book of 1 Samuel with the account of Saul's visiting the witch of Endor in chapter 28. Saul was in a pathetic state. He could no longer seek God's favor and guidance due to his rebellion, so he now turns to a witch, even though he had previously in better days cut off mediums and spiritists from the land in accord with the Torah.

Saul asks the woman to bring up Samuel who had died sometime before. The interpretation of this passage has significant implications for the study of demons and spiritual warfare. We read that, "When the woman saw Samuel, she cried out at the top of her voice and said to Saul, 'Why have you deceived me? you are Saul!'" (v. 12).

Questions abound. Was the medium really able to call up Samuel? Did the author of this text believe that mediums could really call up the spirits of the dead and even the righteous dead? Or is the biblical thrust in general that the claim of mediums to call up the dead are really only contacting deceiving evil spirits who pretend to be the spirits or souls of the departed?

Let us expand the possibilities that arise from this text.

1. Though God forbids spiritism, mediums can call up the spirits of the dead, both the righteous and unrighteous; but this should not be done. On this basis, she was able to call up Samuel, though it was forbidden.

2. Though God forbids spiritism, mediums can call up the spirits of the dead but only the spirits of the lost. Therefore she did not have the normal power to call up Samuel. If it was Samuel, it was by God's overriding decision and power, not her powers.

3. Mediums can only call up pretending evil spirits that pretend to be the spirits of the dead. The spirit that appeared was not really Samuel, but a demonic pretender. Or perhaps God overrode the situation and really sent Samuel.

I do have a view that I think is probable. I do not believe that spiritists (mediums) can call up the spirits of the righteous dead. The Bible teaches that they are in a state of rest and bliss in the presence of God. Even if the picture of Abraham's bosom is a picture of that which was before heaven was opened to the righteous dead (Luke 16:19–26), the picture is one of undisturbed peace. The Bible does not say if, through demonic power, a medium can call up a spirit of an unrighteous dead person. So in general, mediums either are able to only call upon demons that pretend to be the departed person and who would be able to give the kind of information that amazes some of the friends and relatives of the diseased or they can sometimes call up the unrighteous dead (possibilities numbers 2 and 3). My own view is that the medium is usually gaining access to a demon who is pretending to be the departed person (number 3).

I want to make it clear that nothing in this text itself leads to a solution to this problem. Furthermore, I believe that Samuel really did come. The Bible attributes what is said by the figure to Samuel, so it does not fit possibility 2 or 3 above. However, since I have argued that mediums do not have access to the righteous dead, I look at what happened as an intervention of God where He brought Samuel. Here are the reasons.

1. The shock of the women when she saw Samuel. When she saw it was really Samuel, she recognized that King Saul was before her. My sense here is that she was a pretender and that Samuel's coming was beyond her normal experience.

2. Samuel appears as an old man wearing a robe, and Saul thinks that this confirms that it is Samuel. Now why would a spirit look old and be wearing a robe as described? We do not know. Surely in our glorified

and resurrected bodies we will not appear
like this, but the resurrection had not yet
occurred. Samuel's appearance might have
been for Saul's sake, so he would receive
Samuel's words as really from him.

3. Samuel's words are completely in line with
the righteous standards of God and fully
confirm past prophecy, which a demonic
figure would not do.

We learn by this account that there is real danger in the
occult, and there is power. But it is power that no follower
of Yeshua should use.

The Book of 2 Samuel

King David numbers the people

In this strange section, we read the account in
1 Chronicles 21:1 that, "Satan rose up against Israel and
incited David to take a census of Israel." In the account in
2 Samuel 24, we read that the LORD was already angry with
David and incited David to take the census. Apparently
Satan was God's instrument to test David, and David
failed the test. This passage affirms one of the repeated
truths of the Bible; that Satan is ultimately under the control of God.

Exactly why taking a census was a great sin, we do not
know. David does say, "Surely I have sinned, and I have
done wickedly" (2 Sam. 24:17, NKJV). The command was
repulsive to Joab. Although God had previously commanded a census in the days of Moses, there must have
been some command of which we are ignorant or a tradition to not do so. Perhaps God had spoken and said that
Israel was to trust God with military manpower and not

take a census. So perhaps this was a failure to trust God. At any rate, the result was a judgment that diminished the numbers of the fighting men of Israel by seventy thousand, a severe judgment. Amazingly the altar of the LORD that David builds at the end of the plague is the very place where the temple will be built. Here is the account, but abbreviated,

> When the angel stretched out his hand to destroy Jerusalem, the LORD relented concerning the disaster and said to the angel who was afflicting the people, "Enough! Withdraw your hand."
> —2 SAMUEL 24:16

The angel then remained in a state of waiting with a drawn sword extended over Jerusalem. The angel of the LORD then ordered Gad to tell David to build an altar on the threshing floor of Araunah the Jebusite. After paying for the threshing floor, David built the altar as instructed and sacrificed burnt offerings and peace offerings. In the Chronicles account we read that "the LORD answered him with fire from heaven on the altar of burnt offering. Then the LORD spoke to the angel, and he put his sword back in its sheath" (1 Chron. 21:26–27).

These accounts distinguish the LORD (who I believe in other texts is called the Angel, as we argued earlier) and the particular angel who is executing God's judgment. This is important information about angels. God uses them as His instruments of judgment and thus, at least sometimes, acts indirectly through them. The word *angel* is, of course, "messenger"; but it is a messenger of judgment that delivers the judgment.

Excursus

John Warwick Montgomery, *Principalities and Powers*

Dr. Montgomery was known as one of the leading Christian apologists of the last half of the twentieth century and into the twenty-first century, a scholar of scholars.

Now from the distance, out of the bush, came jackal cries, nearer and nearer. The deep growl of the male being answered by the shriller cries of the female.

Suddenly a powerful young man and a splendid young girl, completely naked, leapt over the heads of the onlookers and fell sprawling in the clearing. They sprang up again instantly and started to dance. My God, how they danced! If the dance of the nyanga [the witch doctor] was horrible, this was revolting. They danced the dance of the rutting jackals. As the dance progressed, their imitations became more and more animal, till the horror of it brought the acid of vomit to the throat. Then, in a twinkling, with loathing unbounded, and incredulous amazement, I saw these two turn into jackals before my eyes. The rest of their "act" must be rather imagined than described. Suffice it to say, and I say it with all the authority of long practice of my profession [medicine], no human beings...could have sustained the continued and repeated sexuality of that horrid mating.

Frederick Kaigh, *Witchcraft in Africa*, in John Warwick Montgomery, *Principalities and Powers* (Minneapolis: Bethany House, 1973), 48.

John Warwick Montgomery, *Demon Possession*

Montgomery reports on the *Christian Life Magazine* report in June 1958 on the death of the famous five missionaries to the Auca Indians. The story is immortalized in Elizabeth Elliot's book *Through Gates of Splendor.*

> Indians at Aragjuno mission base knew in a few hours what had happened when five missionaries deep in Ecuador's Auca territory in 1956 failed to make radio contact with anxiously waiting fellow missionaries. How? They asked a local witch doctor. He obliged by falling into a trance, calling up his favorite demons and asking them to tell him where the missing missionaries were. According to the friendly Indians, they heard demons leave the scene and, in a short time, returned with the message that the missionaries were in the Curaray river with Auca lances in them.

> John Warwick Montgomery, *Demon Possession* (Minneapolis, MN: Bethany House, 1976), 210.

C. Peter Wagner, *Spiritual Warfare Strategy*

Dr. Wagner was one of the most important professors of missions in the last half of the twentieth century. For most of his career, he taught at Fuller Theological Seminary in Pasadena, California. He became even more widely known when he supported the ministry of John Wimber, his teaching at Fuller Theological Seminary, and the Vineyard movement of churches.

Here Wagner argues that we can be led by the Spirit, and especially with the help of prophets, to do things that are effective in spiritual warfare though not being clearly enjoined in the New Testament. The rule we should adopt is that nothing can contradict Scripture; but if not explicitly taught against in Scripture or against Scripture principles, it should not be precluded.

> For example, a growing number of us believe that identificational repentance is an extremely vital ingredient in effective strategic level spiritual warfare. When we look for the biblical justification for this, however, we find relatively little about it in the New Testament. We might find bits and pieces here and there, such as the analogy of Jesus' substitutionary atonement; Peter accusing Jews who were on site at the time of crucifying Jesus (Acts 2:36); or some hints in Stephen's speech in Acts 7. Some stress the first-person plural of the Lord's Prayer and argue that "forgive us our sins" could refer to corporate sins. Still, the fact remains that the New Testament contains no outright or explicit teaching about identificational repentance.
>
> The Old Testament, however, contains abundant amounts of material about the principles and practice of identificational repentance....David remitting the sins of Saul against the Gibeonites (see 2 Sam. 21); Nehemiah confessing the sins of his fathers (see Neh. 1:6); ...and Daniel in Daniel 9)....
>
> The question we now face is this: "Where do I along with Critics A and B, get the information that Christians can indeed by demonized and that we should cast demons out of Christians when they are present? Our answers will be similar to the answer Jack Voelkel gave to the same questions in the last chapter:

> - Our personal ministry experience has led us to believe that Christians can be invaded by demons.

- We have arrived at a consensus that this is true from many others who have ministered in the area of deliverance.

- We have seen many positive, even dramatic, results in the lives of those Christians who have been delivered from demons. I would start with my own headache demon I described in the last chapter.

- None of the previous three examples contradicts any biblical teaching.

C. Peter Wagner, *Spiritual Warfare Strategy* (Shippensburg, PA.: Destiny Image, 1976), 76–77, 83.

From an account in early Church history of Gregory the Wonderworker who died 270 AD:

Gregory was highly regarded by his peers for "humility, self-distrust, and practical sense…a man of singular force of character and weighty judgment"….

Gregory's first convert came when, traveling throughout the countryside, he took lodging one night in a notable pagan shrine dedicated to the honor of Apollo. That evening Gregory found himself engaged in spiritual warfare, joined in a fierce battle against the principality who had long ago been invited to occupy that temple. When the shaman or temple priest in charge arrived at the temple the next day, he was surprised that he could get no response from the demon who was usually there. That night, the demon himself appeared to him in a dream and said that he could only return to the temple with Gregory's permission….

"The priest's faith in the god was shattered. Returning to St. Gregory, he became a catechumen,

and subsequently, by holiness of life, proved worthy
to succeed the saint as bishop."

Ibid., 101–102.

Wagner tells the story of Martin of Tours from the early
fourth century. The story is over a spirit that had control
in a village in France.

> In a certain village, he had cast the territorial spirit
> or spirits out of the chief temple and had demol-
> ished the temple itself, as was his custom. But curi-
> ously this did not seem to bother the pagans there as
> much as it had in other places. The reason became
> clear when he discovered that the chief dwelling
> place of the territorial spirit was a nearby pine tree,
> not the temple itself. When Martin started to cut
> down the pine tree, the people rose up against him.
>
> Martin informed them that because the tree had
> been dedicated to the demon, it had to be destroyed.
> Once he had said that, a spokesperson for the group
> confronted Martin and said:
>
> "If you have any trust in thy God, whom you say
> you worship, we ourselves will cut down this tree,
> and be it your part to receive it when falling, for
> if, as you declare, your Lord is with you, you will
> example all injury."
>
> Martin gladly accepted this challenge to enter
> into visible battle against the demonic spirit who
> had been holding these people in captivity for who
> knows how long and who had been greatly enjoying
> their sacrifices and worship....
>
> It so happened that the pine tree had been
> growing decisively in one certain direction, so there
> could be no doubt where it would fall when cut.
> The crowd demanded that Martin stand alone on

the spot where it would certainly fall, which he did. Martin's biographer, Sulpitius Severus, says that the pagans:

"began, therefore, to cut down their own tree with great glee and joyfulness...there was at some distance a great multitude of wondering spectators...the monks at a distance grew pale, expecting only the death of Martin."

But Martin, trusting confidently in the power of God, waited peacefully until the huge tree made a loud cracking noise and began to crash. The then raised his hand against it, acting in the authority of Jesus Christ had given him. Severes says:

"Then, indeed, after the manner of a spinning top (one might have thought it driven back), it swept round to the opposite to such a degree that it almost crushed the rustics who had taken their places there in what was deemed a safe spot." ...

The well-known result was that on that day salvation came to that region.... Not only that village, but the whole region was soon filled with churches and monasteries.

Ibid., 104–106.

Parallel power confrontations are described in subsequent pages 106–110 with the ministries of Benedict of Nursia, the founder of the Benedictines, and Boniface, the missionary to Germany and his confrontation with spirits in trees and temples in the area of Hesse.

Wagner represents Cyprian, Bishop of Carthage.

Relating more directly to strategic level spiritual warfare, Cyprian addresses the phenomenon of demons in idols who "when they are adjured by us in the name of the true God, yield forthwith and confess, and admit they are forced also to leave the bodies (objects) they have invaded."

Ibid., 114.

Wagner reports in the Guatemalan equivalent to *Time Magazine,* the headline,

The Defeat of Maximon: Protestant Fundamentalism Alter the Culture of the Altiplano and Turns the Native Religions into Tourist Attractions. Maximon was a territorial spirit similar to Diana, and he also was defeated essentially through ground-level spiritual warfare.

Prior to the late 1970s, Almolonga was little different from neighboring cities such as Olinte-peque and Zunil. It was characterized by misery, poverty, immorality, corruption, violence, dissension, and disease. Men would typically receive their pay on Friday, spend it on drunken orgies, and return home to distressed wives and children. On Monday, "Drunks were laid out in the streets like cordwood." Many never awoke from their stupors.

The Gospel came to Almolonga in 1951. Thee churches were planted but made virtually no headway. Then a pagan named Mariano Riscajche was saved in 1974, hearing a voice from God, as did Paul, on the day of his conversion, saying, "I have chosen you to serve Me." Soon afterward a sick and demonized man asked Mariano to pray for him, and he was miraculously healed and delivered.

The word got out, more sick came, and many were also healed. Churches began to grow. The opposition to evangelicals then intensified, and unbelieving merchants would not sell food to the Christians. The spiritual battle was on full force.

In 1975, Mariano received a new filling of the Holy Spirit, and began large-scale deliverance, and soon had freed more than 400 people who had been held captive by demons in Almolonga. The spiritual atmosphere of Almolonga began to change radically.

Barrooms closed down. Restaurants and stores and businesses now carry biblical names such as "Bethany," "Jerusalem," and "Shalom." Almolonga has become a city of entrepreneurs who purchase Mercedes trucks, paying cash, to deliver their vegetables on international routes. Families are together and happy. Schools are thriving.

Overlooking a rich valley is 20 evangelical churches. They are the most prominent features of the urban landscape. All of them are alive and well and relatively large. At least 80% of the people of Almolonga are born again Christians.

Ibid., 211–212

Wagner also quotes Yale historian Ramsay MacMullen who believes John ministered in Ephesus after Paul.

John was winning unbelievers to the faith through power ministries such as miraculous healings. But more important than the healings was his personal encounter with Diana.

One day John walked into the huge, ornate temple—one of the wonders of ancient world—and

"in the very temple of [Diana herself], he prayed, 'O God…at whose name every idol takes flight and every demon and every unclean power: now let the demon that is here [in this temple] take flight in Thy name.'"

A more direct power encounter could hardly be imagined…

Dramatic physical manifestations occurred. First, the altar of Diana split into many pieces! Second, half the temple of Diana fell crashing to the ground! Visible spiritual effects also were occurring. According to the record"

"The assembled Ephesians cried out, '[There is but] one God, [the God] of John! ... We are converted, now that we have seen Thy marvelous works!'"

An obvious question arises. Why was it that Paul did not go into the temple of Diana, but John did? The answer is simple because it rests on a principle I have mentioned several times. In strategic spiritual warfare, proceed only on God's timing.

Ibid., 214–215

MacMullen defends this as oral tradition from the second century and probably an accurate transmission.

Chapter 3

SPIRITUAL WARFARE IN KINGS, CHRONICLES, AND THE POST EXILIC BOOKS

SPIRITUAL WARFARE IN KINGS AND CHRONICLES

I F WE WOULD follow the Jewish order of the books of the Bible, we would place First and Second Chronicles at the end of the Hebrew Bible, but since it has so much overlapping material with Kings, we will follow the Christian canonical order. We will mostly follow the books of the Kings and add supplementary material from the Chronicles.

Solomon began well but ended poorly. The theme of the battle against the gods and Israel's compromise with idolatry are prominent themes throughout the books of Kings and Chronicles. One can say that these books are about spiritual warfare and the temptation to syncretism. For Solomon the issue was his loving many foreign women. Israel was told to not intermarry with foreign women since they would turn the hearts of those who marry them to other gods (1 Kings 11:2). Indeed, his wives turned his heart after other gods. Though the text does not say so, there can be real spiritual power in those that worship other gods. Solomon was pleasing his wives by adding their gods to his worship. Here is the sad account,

> He followed Ashtoreth the goddess of the Sidonians,
> and Molek the detestable god of the Ammonites. So
> Solomon did evil in the eyes of the LORD, he did not
> follow the LORD completely, as David his father had
> done. On a hill east of Jerusalem, Solomon built a
> high place for Chemosh the detestable god of Moab
> and for Molek, the detestable god of the Ammonites.
> He did the same for all his foreign wives, who
> burned incense and offered sacrifices to their gods.
>
> —1 KINGS 11:5–8

God's judgment for these acts was to bring war to
Israel. In addition, the kingdom was split after Solomon's
death and his son Rehoboam only ruled Judah—Benjamin
and the tribes of Simeon and Levi who were scattered
throughout Judah.

Jeroboam's reign

Soon after Jeroboam became king of the northern
tribes he set up competing worship centers to Jerusalem
contrary to God's law. This was to prevent his people from
seeking God in Jerusalem. He set up two golden calves,
one in Bethel and one in Dan. He announced them as "the
gods, Israel, who brought you up out of Egypt." It is very
possible that he was making a representation of YHWH,
the LORD. He also established alternative festivals and
altars at high places.

In chapter 13 a pattern is established that will be
repeated over and over. It is the theme of prophetic opposition to the compromised syncretism and to worshipping
the false gods of the land of Canaan and other nations. We
are not told the name of this first prophet in a series, but
he is called a man of God from Judah. Sometimes as in
this case, there is a direct power confrontation with God.

This is the word from the prophet,

> He cried out against the altar by the word of the Lord. "O altar, altar! Thus says the Lord. 'Behold, a child, Josiah by name, shall be born to the house of David; and on you he shall sacrifice the priests of the high places who burn incense on you, and men's bones shall be burned on you.'" And he gave a sign the same day, saying, "This is the sign which the LORD has spoken: Surely the altar shall split apart, and the ashes on it shall be poured out." So it came to pass when King Jeroboam heard the saying of the man of God, who cried out against the altar in Bethel, that he stretched out his hand from the altar, saying, "Arrest him!" Then his hand, which he stretched out toward him, withered, so that he could not pull it back to himself. The altar also was split apart, and the ashes poured out from the altar, according to the sign which the man of God had given by the word of the LORD.
>
> —1 KINGS 13:2–5, NKJV

After the king asked the man of God to intercede for him, the king's hand was restored. However, Jeroboam did not repent and continued to consecrate as priests whoever desired the role. The chapter concludes with these words, "This thing was the sin of the house of Jeroboam, so as to exterminate and destroy it from the face of the earth" (v. 34, NKJV).

I note the fulfillment in Josiah slaughtering the priests of the high place of Bethel and burning the human bones on the altar to defile it. **Prophetic speaking that comes to pass sometime later in the future can be a significant part of spiritual warfare.**

The stories of the northern tribes and Judah are very sad. While there were more good kings in Judah, the reality of idolatry and heinous occult practices led to the downfall of both kingdoms. These practices included cult prostitution and child sacrifice. We can ask why Israel would fall into such evil. The answer is that there was a deeply held belief that when they engaged in such practices they experienced real power and that these powers could be entreated or manipulated for their protection and prosperity. Yet, such practices bring the judgment of God. Though the text does not yet say it, the total witness of the Bible is that these practices bring demonic oppression and ultimately possession.

The power encounter of Elijah

The greatest power encounter in the Hebrew Bible is in 1 Kings 18, the famous confrontation of Elijah with the prophets of Baal. This is a confrontation in the context of the northern tribes during the time of King Ahab and Queen Jezebel.

Elijah confronts the prophets of Baal with a contest and the people agree. They each are to make altars and are then to call on the name of their gods—or God in Elijah's case. "The God who answers by fire, He is God" (v. 24, NKJV). In these contests—which are known as well in world missions where there are confrontations with witches, warlocks, and shamans—the God of Israel wins and the power of the false gods is bound. There are too many examples to adequately describe! Elijah taunts the false prophets and says that maybe their god is sleeping and needs to be awakened or maybe he has gone on a journey. They cut themselves to get their god to intervene.

Then Elijah drenches his altar with water and makes it more unlikely that any mere natural event could be the explanation of what will happen. At the time of the sacrifice, he calls upon the LORD, God of Abraham, Isaac and Israel. He says, "Hear me, O LORD, hear me, that this people may know that You are the LORD God, and that You have turned their hearts back to You again" (v. 37, NKJV).

Then the fire of the LORD fell, licked up the water and burned the wood, stones and soil. After this the drought ended. In spite of this, Jezebel the queen does not repent, but vows to kill Elijah. Whether there was spiritual power operating in her, or merely disappointment and fear in Elijah, or both, we do not know. That Ahab and Jezebel do not turn to God but all the more turn against God and Elijah is one of the sad aspects of spiritual warfare, namely that people can choose against God in spite of the evidence.

Ahab defeats King Ben-Hadad of Syria

In 1 Kings 20 we read of the account of Israel's defeat of the Syrian King Ben-Hadad. In this case there is no great spiritual warfare preparation, but the prophetic word is a judgment of God because they were challenging God's sovereignty. There were two defeats. The second battle is even more noteworthy. God told the king of Israel:

> Because the Arameans think the LORD is a god of the hills and not a god of the valleys, I will deliver this vast army into your hands and you will know that I am the LORD.
>
> —1 KINGS 20:28

A great victory for Israel followed.

Joram the king of Israel and Jehoshaphat the king of Judah defeat Moab

In 2 Kings 3:1–27 we read another account of supernatural power in war. Jehoshaphat agrees to an alliance with Joram (Jehoram). The King of Edom is allied with them. As they go forth to fight Moab they run out of water. Then they inquire of the prophet Elisha. Elisha is at first unwilling to prophecy into this unholy alliance, but then says,

> As surely as the LORD Almighty lives, whom I serve, if I did not have respect for the presence of Jehoshaphat king of Judah, I would not look at you or even notice you.
>
> —2 KINGS 3:14

so he can hear from God telepheny

Elisha called for a harpist. As he played the hand of the LORD came upon him and he said,

> Thus says the Lord: "Make this valley full of ditches." For thus says the LORD: "You will not see wind, nor shall you see rain; yet that valley shall be filled with water, so that you, your cattle, and your animals may drink. This is a simple matter in the sight of the LORD; He will also deliver the Moabites into your hand."
>
> —2 KINGS 3:16–18, NKJV

The Moabites had heard that the armies were coming and looked out in the early morning from their city. The water looked red, like blood. Therefore they thought the armies slaughtered each other so they went out to plunder. However, they were deceived and Israel rose up and slaughtered them. The allied armies destroyed towns and fields. As they went to conquer his city, the king of Moab sacrificed his firstborn son on the city wall. Following this a fierce battle ensued, so much so that Israel, Judah, and Edom withdrew and returned to their own land.

Now this raises interesting question. Was it God's will that Israel and Judah only get so far and not fully conquer the leading city? Was it due to the compromised alliance with Edom? Did the Moabite king's sacrifice actually release supernatural evil power for war or did it simply motivate his people? The text is silent on all these possible interpretations.

Again, we see that these texts in the historical books of the Bible are models that have implications for spiritual warfare because the wars of ancient Israel are both real physical wars and spiritual warfare. In this case there is victory because of a righteous man, King Jehoshaphat. **So we learn the principle that the righteousness of the one doing the war is crucial in gaining a victory.**

Jehoshaphat defeats Moab and Ammon

The account of the war between Judah and Moab and Ammon is noteworthy. It has often been used as an illustration of spiritual warfare. In 2 Chronicles we read of the account. When Jehoshaphat was told that a vast army was coming against him and was already at En Gedi, we read, "Alarmed, Jehoshaphat resolved to inquire of the LORD, and he proclaimed a fast for all Judah" (20:3).

The king gathered people from all over Judah to the temple and prayed to God. His prayer is a model of dependence on God, appeal to His promises, and humility before His throne. The answer came in prophecy through Jahaziel, the son of Zechariah, who was a Levite with prophetic gifting. Jehoshaphat was told that the battle is the LORD's not his. In this particular battle praise and worship defeated the enemy. We read,

They [the singers] went out at the head of the army saying, "Give thanks to the Lord, for his love endures forever." As they began to sing and praise, the Lord set ambushes against the men of Ammon and Moab and Mount Seir who were invading Judah, and they were defeated. The men of Ammon and Moab rose up against the men from Mount Seir to destroy and annihilate them. After they finished slaughtering the men from Seir, they helped to destroy one another. When the men of Judah came to the place that overlooks the desert and looked toward the vast army, they saw only dead bodies lying on the ground; no one had escaped. So Jehoshaphat and his men went to carry off their plunder, and they found among them a great amount of equipment and clothing and also articles of value—more than they could take away. There was so much plunder that it took three days to collect it. On the fourth day they assembled in the Valley of Berakah, where they praised the Lord. This is why it is called the Valley of Berakah to this day.

—2 Chronicles 20:21–28

They returned to Jerusalem and went to the temple with musical instruments. Then the results are given in the text.

The fear of God came on all the surrounding kingdoms when they heard how the Lord had fought against the enemies of Israel. And the kingdom of Jehoshaphat was at peace, for his God had given him rest on every side.

—2 Chronicles 20:29–30

Again, we see a great example of spiritual warfare, not carried on by commanding evil powers but by the worship of a committed people whereby the presence of God and His intervention destroyed the enemies of Israel. We do not know if angels were involved in the events, but it is not improbable though the text is silent on this.

When Israel is unfaithful and falls into idolatry, she is defeated by her enemies. This pattern repeats itself again and again.

King of Syria

The account of the war between Aram and Israel

The story is in 2 Kings 6:8–23. In verse 13 we find that the king of Aram (Syria) had surrounded the city of Dothan where the king of Israel was staying. Elisha's servant asked, "What shall we do?" (v. 15). Elisha answered,

> "Don't be afraid"….Those who are with us are more than those who are with them. And Elisha prayed, "Open his eyes, LORD, so that he may see." Then the LORD opened the servant's eyes, and he looked and saw the hills full of horses and chariots of fire all around Elisha.

angelic armies

> 2 KINGS 6:16-17

When Elijah was taken up to heaven, a chariot of fire appeared and separated Elijah from Elisha and Elijah went up to heaven in the whirlwind. Elisha saw this and cried out, "My father! My father! The chariots and horsemen of Israel" (2:12).

The idea seems to be that of a heavenly army which gives content to the often-used phrase, "the LORD of hosts." The idea of angelic armies is little described in the Hebrew Bible texts but may be assumed in other biblical texts.

a non righteous King

Jehoash defeats the Arameans (Syrians)

In this particular story found in 2 Kings 13:14–20, a king who was not righteous was nevertheless called to defeat the king of Syria. In this case, prophetic action in symbol by the king through the command of the prophet Elisha is a key to what will happen in the war. He is told to shoot an arrow through the east window of the prophet's house and when he does so,

> Elisha declared, "The LORD's arrow of victory over Aram! ... You will completely destroy the Arameans at Aphek." Then he said, "Take the arrows," and the king took them. Elisha told him, "Strike the ground." He struck it three times and stopped. The man of God was angry with him and said, "You should have struck the ground five or six times; then you would have defeated Aram and completely destroyed it. But now you will defeat it only three times."
>
> —2 KINGS 13:17–19

In this case the intensity of the action of the king determined the level of victory. So here we see that a prophetic symbolic action can be determinative in warfare. It is prophetic action by the word of Elisha. **Again, I see a principle that an accurate prophetic word enjoining prophetic symbolic action can be determinate in spiritual warfare.**

Hezekiah and the Assyrian invasion

As prophesied through Isaiah in chapter 7 of his book and recorded in 2 Kings 18:17–19:37, the Assyrians conquered most of Israel and Judah. The latter was a judgment on Hezekiah's father, King Ahaz, and his alliance with Assyria. However, Hezekiah turned to the LORD and was ultimately delivered. The account of warfare is quite astonishing and is archaeologically confirmed by the stele of Sennacherib. The challenge of the Assyrian leaders is not only to Hezekiah but also to God. The commander of the Assyrian armies says,

> Do not listen to Hezekiah, for he is misleading you when he says, "The Lord will deliver us." Has the god of any nation every delivered his land from the hand of the king of Assyria? Where are the gods of Hamath and Arpad? Where are the gods of Sepharvaim, Hena and Ivva? Have they rescued Samaria from my hand? Who of all the gods of these countries has been able to save his land from me? How then can the LORD deliver Jerusalem from my hand?
>
> —2 KINGS 18:32–35

King Hezekiah humbled himself, put on sackcloth, and went to the prophet Isaiah. Isaiah then prophesies the deliverance of Judah. He calls the words of the commander blasphemy. The king of Assyria will be cut down with the sword.

Again Sennacherib sent another message to Hezekiah. It repeated the same claim and called for Judah to surrender. Hezekiah received the letter and he went up to the temple, spread it out before the LORD, and prayed. He then called upon God to deliver them "so that all kingdoms of the earth may know that you alone, LORD, are God" (19:19).

Again, Isaiah prophecies their utter defeat. God has heard the prayer of the king. We read,

> That night the angel of the LORD went out and put to death a hundred and eighty-five thousand men in the Assyrian camp. When the people got up the next morning, there were all the dead bodies! So

63

> Sennacherib king of Assyria broke camp and withdrew. He returned to Nineveh and stayed there.
>
> —2 KINGS 19:35–36

Subsequently, back in Nineveh, as he worshiped in his pagan temple his sons cut him down with the sword.

So in this case, it was earnest prayer to God for deliverance from a blaspheming invader. Here we read of the involvement of **an angel of judgment.** This great account therefore **establishes intercession in spiritual warfare just as the previous one establishes worship.**

As for angels, as we come to the end of these historical books that mostly detail Israel's history before the exile (586 BC), we do find very brief descriptions of angelic figures, but very little information on their roles, extent of power, or any hierarchies among them.

POST-EXILIC HISTORICAL BOOKS

The books of Ezra and Nehemiah have no significant content on angels or demons. The spiritual warfare is in the context of concrete action. In the case of Ezra, is it to get the people to repent of their intermarriages and compromise. Certainly such purification has spiritual warfare dimensions, for to be purified from sin through repentance is to be freed from demonic influence; but nothing is said about that.

Also in the Book of Nehemiah, there is nothing made of demonic powers. The opposition is human, enemies that seek to destroy the restoration of the Jewish people to significant power in their own land, though they will be subject to the Persians. Many spiritual people have seen the story of Nehemiah in rebuilding the walls of Jerusalem as an analogy to the kind of war we fight to establish the work of God and to extend His Kingdom. Wisdom in facing opposition to God's work can be gleaned from this wonderful book. In addition, the need to drive away people who would compromise the people of God is a conclusive ending of the book.

> One of the sons of Johaida son of Elishib the high priest was son-in-law to Sanballat the Horonite. And I drove him away from me. Remember them, my God, because they defiled the priestly office and the covenant of the priesthood and of the Levites. So I purified the priests and the Levites of everything foreign, and assigned them duties, each to his own task. I also made provision for contributions of wood at designated times, and for the firstfruits.
>
> —NEHEMIAH 13:28–31

The Book of Esther is controversial. Some think it is more of an historical novelette that is based on historical information with regard to a danger to the Jewish nation, and others think it is strictly historical. We will not deal with this controversy.

The book does not mention angels, demons, or even God directly. Yet, the providence of God permeates the book. The book certainly shows spiritual warfare at its height. What could be a more intense spiritual war than a war to destroy the Jewish people and to thwart the plan of God for the redemption of the world through the Jewish people. The one aspect of spiritual warfare is the fast that was undertaken by the people before Esther approached the king to find mercy for her people.

Excursus

Norman Grubb, *Rees Howells, Intercessor*

I consider Rees Howells one of the greatest intercessors and leaders in spiritual warfare of modern times. This classic book is a foundation of my understanding of what is possible in prayer. This section of the book shows spiritual warfare as part of fighting an actual war, World War II. The book shows the astonishing effects of prayer led by Rees Howells at his Welsh Bible School. There are from journals of prayer recorded at the time.

> From this time on, through all the years of the war, the whole College was in prayer every evening from seven o'clock to midnight, with only a brief interval for supper....
>
> May 22, 9 a.m. "The world is in a panic today, and certainly we would be too, unless were quite sure the Lord has spoken to us. The destiny of England will be at stake today and to-morrow." ...
>
> May 26 was the day of public prayer in Britain....
>
> On May 28 Mr. Howells again was alone with God. In the meetings the prayer was for God to intervene at Dunkirk and save our men; and as the Spirit came upon them in prayer and supplication, what one prayed at the end expressed the assurance given to all: "I feel sure something has happened."
>
> May 29 was the day of the evacuation of Dunkirk. Mr. Howells said, "Let us be dear in our prayer that the intercession is gained. The battle is the Holy Spirit's. See Him outside of yourselves tonight. He is there on the battle filed with His drawn sword."

May 30, 7:80 p.m. "From a worldly standpoint there is no hope of victory; but God has said it. I could not come tonight and ask Him to intervene, because we have already said that He is going to intervene. Instead of bad news about our soldiers, if he is on the field of battle, He can change that and make it very good news. Oh, for God to lift us up tonight! ...We state in the strongest terms: The enemy will not invade Christian England."

...Remembering the miracle of Dunkirk, acknowledged by our leaders to be an intervention from God, the calm sea allowing the smallest boats to cross, the almost complete evacuation of our troops, and then the lead Mr. Churchill gave to this nation, how thankful we are that God had this company of hidden intercessors, whose lives were on the altar day after day as they stood in the gap for the deliverance of Britain."

..."The director opened his message by saying first thing the Lord has told him that morning was, 'Pray that Moscow will not fall!' It seemed ridiculously impossible for we had heard that its fall was inevitable; but although the prayer was so far beyond us, yet the Spirit 'laid it on us...so we travailed all day, until the late meeting that night, He so inspired us through His servant that we had the assurance that God was answering. The Lord gave liberty to pray that the Nazis might be utterly overthrown in a Russian winter. We shall never forget the joy of victory. He gave us faith mounted up during those days." ...We all know the end of the story; Moscow never fell, and Goering, recounting later the misfortunes of that winter, stated that three million of the flower of the Nazi army perished in the snow. Victor Kravchenko in his book, *I Chose Freedom*, said:

"The Germans could have taken Moscow those days virtually without a struggle. Why they turned back is a mystery only the Germans themselves can solve for history."

God now began to turn the prayers of the College into yet another direction...prayer began to be centered on the Bible Lands. This was really one of the main burdens of prayer at the College, because long before, God had revealed to them that this was not just a European war, but that through it, "in the determinate counsel and foreknowledge of God," the Jews would return to Palestine, the Gospel go out to every creature, and the Savior be able to return. Thus as soon as the Bible Land seemed in danger of invasions, God turned their prayer in that direction. "I am sure, "said Mr. Howells, "the enemy will never touch Palestine, Syria and Iraq."

The area of greatest immediate danger was North Africa. With the appearance of Rommel and the German armoured divisions there, the menace to Egypt became grave; and if Egypt fell, the door was wide open to Palestine....

"Unless God will intervene on behalf of Palestine," said Mr. Howells, on July 4, 1942, "there will be no safety there for the Jews. These Bible Lands must be protected, because it is to these lands the Saviour will come back.... Don't let Alexandria be taken, but give Rommel a setback." ..."Is this the prayer we prayed this afternoon of the Holy Ghost, that the enemy is not to take Alexandria? I am speaking to all of you who took a real part in the prayers against the enemy, praying him down to the Mediterranean, praying him to Russia, keeping him out of Moscow! ...We can be...sure of the enemy not taking Alexandria." ...

That evening Mr. Howells and the College came through to victory...."I know now he will never take Egypt—neither Alexandria nor Cairo will fall." ...

The following week...on that very Saturday when the extra prayer meeting was called, it was over that week-end that the tide turned at El Alamein, and Alexandria was saved.

Norman Grubb, *Rees Howells, Intercessor* (Cambridge, UC: Lutterworth Press, 1973), 254–256.

Francis Frangipane, *The Three Battlegrounds*

In a clear and powerful presentation, Francis Frangipane writes of the three battlegrounds of spiritual warfare: the mind, the Church, and heavenly places. The following excepts are from the third, heavenly places.

God uses the church community as one body fused together in the fire of Christ's love. He would have us praying together, working and building our churches in the Spirit of His Kingdom. No one knows the local battle better than the local pastors....

[In New Testament times] the pastors [elders of a city]...were accountable both to God and to each other; a true plurality of leadership in each community. The city-wide church, as God sees it, would be free from jealousy, "sheep stealing" and personal ambition. It would truly be one body.... Personal ambition is the motive of the Antichrist; it is the name of the stronghold that has made us divided....

Therefore, when you meet with Christians from other churches, come as their servants and look to bless them....

During the 1970's I pastored in an organization which had scores of men who functioned in the revelation gifts of wisdom and knowledge. There was "day and night" prayer, beautiful worship, commitment and power....There seemed to be no curse or omen that worked against us; God have given us his blessing, success seemed inevitable. But as...with the daughters of Moab, so the spirit of Jezebel launched its attack upon this work of God.

If the enemy cannot attack you directly, he will seek to bring you into sin, thereby positioning you under the judgments of God. When the Jezebel spirit began to manifest itself, and tolerance toward sexual sins increased, I approached the founder of the movement with my concerns. Meeting with him privately, I entreated him as a son does a father; but he dismissed me. Three months later I approached him again, appealing this time to the entire governmental team which was with him, warning them with tears that the judgment of the Lord against tolerating Jezebel was sickness and death (Revelation 2:22–23). Once more I was dismissed. Several months later I was removed from leadership, and then, ultimately, forced from the group. Within months after I left the leader divorced his wife, and less than a year later he married his secretary. Within two years he was dead from prostate cancer.

The impact of this experience was both devastating and enlightening. Even though I personally went through a period of great discouragement and self-doubt, I learned much about Jezebel and the sin of presumption. I saw that grown men assume God will not judge them, it is only a matter of time before the tempter comes to destroy them. It is significant that, while Jesus had the spirits of wisdom and understanding, counsel, strength and knowledge, His *delight* was "**in the fear of the Lord**" (Is. 11:2–3). The sin of presumption is the antithesis of the fear of the Lord. It is the harbinger of future defeat.

Francis Frangipane, *The Three Battlegrounds* (Cedar Rapids, IA: Advancing Church Publications, 1989), 95–96, 141–142.

Chapter 4

SPIRITUAL WARFARE IN THE PSALMS AND THE PROPHETS

SPIRITUAL WARFARE IN THE PSALMS

THE PSALMS PROVIDE us little in the way of information on angels and demons. They do provide a wealth of information on how the psalmists prayed in situations of great trial and danger. They do not address powers of darkness, but appeal to God to vanquish human enemies. Calling upon God to vanquish human enemies is very common in the Psalms. The interpreter has to show great care in applying the Psalms to the way we pray today. Our call to love our enemies seems inconsistent with many of the expressions in the Psalms that call for God to take vengeance. However, was God simply allowing the recording of the psalmists' expressions without endorsing their full content? Is there a place for prayer for God's severe judgment on enormous human powers of evil (e.g., the Nazis of World War II or the Islamic State Terrorist people and organization)? Psalms are not always prescriptive examples. Yet, many have seen in the Psalms a pattern that can be prayed in warfare with the demonic realm. The demonic is not a realm of enemies for which we pray, nor are we called to love these enemies.

The Psalms affirm the reality of angels but sparsely. Psalm 8 informs us that mankind was made "a little lower than heavenly beings [angels] and crowned him with glory and honor" (Psa. 8:5, ESV). Mankind is to be the ruler over God's works, so mankind is to someday attain higher elevation.

One interesting reference is found in Psalm 106:36–38, which speaks of the compromise of the Israelites with the Canaanites.

> They worshipped their idols, which became a snare to them. They sacrificed their sons and their daughters to false Gods [demons]. They shed innocent blood, the blood of their sons and daughters, whom they sacrificed to the idols of Canaan, and the land was desecrated by their blood.

This is an early passage indicating that there was an understanding that pagan sacrifices were sacrifices to demons, which is later stated by Paul in the New Testament.

THE PRE-EXILIC PROPHETS

I will seek to survey the prophetic books in historical order. The constant message is that Israel reaps the judgment of God due to idolatry and injustice. There is also a continual theme of ultimate redemption. Despite Israel's unfaithfulness, somehow God enabled them to be restored and to ultimately succeed.

The Book of Hosea

An example of this theme from Hosea is instructive.

> They set up kings without my consent; they choose princes without my approval. With their silver and gold they make idols for themselves to their own destruction. Samaria, throw out your calf idol!

My anger burns against them. How long will they be incapable of purity? They are from Israel! This calf—a metalworker has made it; it is not God. It will be broken in pieces, that calf of Samaria. They sow to the wind and reap the whirlwind. The stalk has no head; it will produce no flour. Were it to yield grain, foreigners would swallow it up. Israel is swallowed up; now she is among the nations like something no one wants. For they have gone up to Assyria like a wild donkey wondering alone. Ephraim has sold herself to lovers.

—Hosea 8:4–9

Only a remnant of the northern tribes would find deliverance by joining the south, but the southern tribes would also rebel and fall into idolatry. Idol worship is an occult power.

Pagan worship sometimes used cult prostitution as a way to connect to the gods. The Bible does not say what happens to such persons in terms of demonization or possession. This would be a New Covenant understanding. However, note these strong words,

They sacrifice on the mountaintops and burn offerings on the hills, under oak, poplar and terebinth, where the shade is pleasant. Therefore your daughters turn to prostitution and your daughters-in-law to adultery. I will not punish your daughters when they turn to prostitution, nor your daughters-in-law when they commit adultery, because the men themselves consort with harlots and sacrifice with shrine prostitutes—a people without understanding will come to ruin!

—Hosea 4:13–14

Again, the Hebrew Bible does not say much about what happens to people who engage in such practices, but in the New Covenant Scriptures we find that it corrupts the inner being of the person. So spiritual warfare in the prophetic books is, as in the historical books (also prophetic), a constant battle between syncretism and compromise where the people of God lose their power and eventually their national independence.

The answer is also found in the conclusion of Hosea,

> Take words with you and return to the Lord. Say to him: "Forgive all our sins and receive us graciously, that we may offer the fruit of our lips..... We will never again say, 'Our gods' to what our own hands have made."
>
> —Hosea 14:2–3

The way back requires a supernatural healing for God says,

> I will heal their waywardness, and love them freely, for my anger has turned away from them. I will be like the dew to Israel; he will blossom like a lily. Like a cedar of Lebanon he will send down his roots; his young shoots will grow. His splendor will be like an olive tree, his fragrance like a cedar of Lebanon.
>
> —Hosea 14:4–6

The Book of Joel

In Joel the great locust plague is a manifestation of judgment. A holy fast is called. Great repentance is needed. So we see that depth of repentance and fasting is part of deliverance for the nation. It can be the key to deliverance and spiritual warfare at all times of great trial and judgment. We read,

"Even now," declares the LORD, "return to me with all your heart, with fasting and weeping and mourning." Rend your heart and not your garments. Return to the LORD your God, for he is gracious and compassionate, slow to anger and abounding in love, and he relents from sending calamity.

—JOEL 2:12–13

Joel tells us that this approach was successful. The locust plague in the days of Joel is then used as a prophetic analogy for the last great judgment that is to come. This is the last great spiritual battle, the war of good and evil at its height. However, it will be the time of a great outpouring of the Spirit (2:28–32). It will lead to the final and ultimate deliverance of Judah (3:20–21)

The Book of Amos

In Amos the theme of social justice (not defined in the Bible as unqualified equality as in Marxism) is very strong. The nations are judged on the basis of justice as are Israel and Judah. Yet ultimate restoration is promised. Returning fully to the Lord, repentance, and following His ways are at the center of spiritual warfare.

The Book of Obadiah

In Obadiah the battle is between the Edomites and God's people. We read,

But on Mount Zion there shall be deliverance, And there shall be holiness; The house of Jacob shall possess their inheritance.

—OBADIAH 1:17, NKJV

The only spiritual warfare we see in this small book is faith in the promise of God.

77

The Book of Jonah

In Jonah if we are to look at the theme of spiritual warfare, it consists in preaching a message of the warning of judgment leading to repentance. By that message, Nineveh repented and was delivered. **This is an important aspect of spiritual warfare as individuals, communities, and nations are confronted with sin and called upon to repent.**

The Book of Micah

Micah again repeats the same themes. Disobedience to God brings judgment, but repentance and genuine turning back brings restoration. The ultimate restoration is pronounced, even leading to the redemption of the whole world. Again spiritual warfare is in terms of the preaching of the word of repentance that leads to deliverance from oppression and restoration.

All of this leads me to emphasize at this point **that many who seek to do spiritual warfare and even deliverance ministry for individuals are weak in the message of repentance and a full return to God and submission to His ways. Just casting out demons, or praying for healing of negative experiences, or finally addressing the powers of darkness, will be in effective without a strong message of righteousness and repentance.**

The Book of Nahum

Nahum pronounces the judgment on Nineveh, the Assyrians, but also announces the restoration of the splendor of Israel. Israel's nemesis will finally be judged.

We will not continue in historical order so we might cover the last two of the shorter prophetic books.

The Book of Habakkuk

Habakkuk addresses God's strange mode of spiritual warfare. The nation of Babylon (named for her capital city) will destroy Judah. The prophet is stunned since Babylon is more wicked than Judah. How can this be God's way? Yet this terrible judgment will purify the people of God who will later be restored from captivity and freed from gross external idolatry once and for all. The only answer in such a situation is to stand in faith that God is good and that His purpose will lead to the right ends. The way of deliverance for the righteous is to live by faith/faithfulness. So standing in faith/faithfulness is an important ingredient of spiritual warfare.

Ultimately our faith is in the fulfillment of God's promises, and Habakkuk repeats the promise given by Isaiah, "For the earth will be filled With the knowledge of the Lord, As the waters cover the sea" (2:14, nkjv).

This is a promise of world redemption.

The Book of Zephaniah

Finally, Zephaniah, the last of the pre-exilic prophets, warns about God's proximate judgment on Judah and the ultimate judgment to come on the whole world, the awesome and terrible Day of the Lord. The way of protection in the coming judgment is summarized in chapter 2:3.

> Seek the Lord, all you humble of the land, you who do what he commands. Seek righteousness, seek humility; perhaps you will be sheltered on the day of the Lord's anger.

A righteous remnant will be delivered and the nations will come to the knowledge of the Lord.

The Book of Isaiah

The Book of Isaiah continues the same theme of Israel's corruption through the practice of idolatry. The idea that there is spiritual power of a negative kind in idolatry while at the same time the idol itself is a powerless statue expresses the same paradox as we find in many of the Hebrew texts.

Isaiah's calling introduces us to angelic beings in the presence of God. In chapter 6 Isaiah says that he saw the LORD seated on a throne. Above Him were seraphs, each with six wings.

> With two wings they covered their faces, with two they covered their feet, and with two they were flying. And they were calling to one another, "Holy, holy, holy is the LORD Almighty, the whole earth is full of his glory."
>
> —ISAIAH 6:2

One of the seraphs took a coal from the altar and touched Isaiah's lips. Awesome angelic figures are before God's throne.

Isaiah 14 includes one section that has been understood in historical interpretation to give us information about Satan. The context is a prophecy against Babylon, the nation used as an instrument of judgment against Judah. I quote the text here:

> How you have fallen from heaven, morning star, son of the dawn! You have been cast down to the earth, you who once laid low the nations! You said in your heart, "I will ascend to heavens; I will raise my throne above the stars of God; I will sit enthroned on the mount of assembly, on the utmost heights of

Mount Zaphon. I will ascend above the tops of the clouds; I will make myself like the Most High." But you are brought down to the dead, to the depths of the pit. Those who see you stare at you, they ponder your fate: "Is this the man who shook the earth, and made kingdoms tremble."

—Isaiah 14:12–16

Some interpreters think that these verses are descriptive of the king of Babylon. He was so self-exalted. We recall the pride of King Nebuchadnezzar recorded in the Book of Daniel and his period of insanity after he was judged by God. Ancient kings of the east did indeed exalt themselves in very inflated terms. However, the king of Babylon was not cast down in this way until the last Babylonian king, Balthazar. Therefore, most classical interpreters see the text as going beyond the description of the Babylonian king to the model of pride rooted in the devil himself. The text addresses him as if he really was in God's presence— "morning star, son of the dawn." His being cast down to earth fits the fall of a creature who is not of this world. Indeed, the Book of Revelation uses this text when it speaks of Satan being cast down to the earth. Some interpreters use this text to describe Satan before his fall as the leader of God's holy angelic choirs, though this is more speculative. The name Lucifer is derived from this text, the Son of the Morning.

These interpretations certainly make sense. However, the idea that the text is hyperbolic for the Babylonian king(s) and the ultimate fall of the Babylonian dynasty is also a possibility.

My own view is that both are intentionally conjoined and the Babylonian king is addressed in terms that reflect the spirit of the one he followed—Lucifer.

Verses in Isaiah 24 indicate that the power of kings on earth is connected to the powers in the heavens. This seems to anticipate New Testament teaching about principalities and powers.

> In that day the LORD will punish the powers in the heavens above and the kings on the earth below. They will be herded together like prisoners bound in a dungeon; they will be shut up in prison and be punished after many days.
>
> —ISAIAH 24:21–22

One text in particular speaks in terms that reflect the idea of a power of darkness, Isaiah 26:21–27:2. I believe this is a very important text and the first to give a larger picture of the devil. The picture of the snake in Genesis 3 does not describe a powerful prince of darkness. It is not close to the later images in the Hebrew texts or in the New Covenant Scriptures. This text speaks about God punishing the people of the earth for their sins and the earth disclosing the blood shed upon her. The idea of the blood of the innocent who were slain crying out for justice is an old image going back to the slaying of Abel. The text then goes on to speak about the punishment of a sea serpent called Leviathan.

> In that day, the LORD will punish with his sword— his great and powerful sword—Leviathan the gliding serpent, Leviathan the coiling serpent; he will slay the monster of the sea.
>
> —ISAIAH 27:1

Scholars point out that the sea represents people. This giant serpent dwells in the midst of the peoples of the earth and must be punished or slain. This passage provides us with an image which will be carried forward into the New Covenant Scriptures and greatly expands the idea of the snake in Genesis 3.

The idea of fierce sea monsters that live in the oceans was a common mythological theme in the ancient world. Using such an image as a metaphor for a great power of evil that dwells in the midst of the people of the earth and that exercises great sway over nations is a new and powerful image. There is nothing in the text that tells us what we should do about it. The text only promises that God will deal with it.

After God, the Lord, does deal with it, we are told that God's vine, Israel, will come into prosperity. "Jacob will take root, Israel will bud and blossom and fill all the world with fruit" (27:6).

The Books of Jeremiah and Ezekiel

These two important prophetic books record the words of the prophets before the first great exile of the Jewish people and the end of the first commonwealth. Jeremiah ministers in the land of Israel and Ezekiel in the land of Babylon with the first population that was taken captive. Their ministry continues past the destruction of the first temple in Jerusalem and the destruction of the city of Jerusalem.

The Book of Jeremiah continues the theme of spiritual warfare in the sense of the battle against idolatry and compromise. The way of deliverance is by repentance and returning to God in response to the word of the prophet. Sadly, the prophet's word was mostly not heeded and led to the terrible destruction and captivity of the southern tribes.

Ezekiel provides us with several angelic visions. The main one is first described in chapter 1, where he has a vision of a chariot with four living creatures. We read their description,

> In appearance their form was human, but each of them had four faces and four wings. Their legs were straight; their feet were like those of a calf and gleamed like burnished bronze. Under their wings on their four sides they had human hands. All four of them had faces and wings, and the wings of one touched the wings of another. Each one went straight ahead; they did not turn as they moved.
>
> —Ezekiel 1:5–9

I believe that this vision is parallel to the cherubim that were beside the ark in the temple. The vision continues with amazing symbolism. The key is not to try to describe what these beings looked like but what the description symbolizes.

> Their faces looked like this: Each of the four had the face of a human being, and on the right side each had the face of a lion, and on the left the face of an ox, each also had the face of an eagle. Such were their faces. They each had two wings spreading out upward, each wing touching that of the creature on either side, and each had two other wings covering its body. Each one went straight ahead. Wherever the spirit would go, they would go, without turning as they went. The appearance of the living creatures was like burning coals of fire or like torches. Fire moved back and forth among the creatures; it was bright, and lightning flashed out of it. The creatures sped back and forth.
>
> —Ezekiel 1:10–14

Then Ezekiel saw a wheel on the ground beside each creature. There is a detailed description of these wheels. There is an expanse over the heads of the living creatures. The sound of the wings under the expanse was like the voice of God or the tumult of an army. A voice was heard above the expanse. Above the expanse was a throne and a figure like that of a man. It was the appearance of the likeness of the glory of God.

For our purpose, while it is difficult to fully account for what this is all about, to say the least, the point is that angelic beings are in the very place by the very throne of God. This will again be described in a different way in the Book of Revelation. The angelic figures worship and are part of the awesome majesty of the LORD on His throne.

In Ezekiel chapter 8, the description of pagan practices, even brought into the temple, must have brought terrible grief to the prophet and those who sought to be faithful to the covenant of God with Israel.

> Son of man, have you seen what the elders of the house of Israel are doing in the darkness, each at the shrine of his own idol? They say, "The LORD does not see us; the LORD has forsaken the land." ... Then he brought me to the entrance of the north gate of the house of the LORD, and I saw women sitting there, mourning for the god Tammuz.... He then brought me into the inner court of the house of the LORD, and there at the entrance of to the temple, between the portico and the altar, were about twenty-five men. With their backs toward the temple of the LORD and their faces toward the east, they were bowing down to the sun in the east.
>
> —EZEKIEL 8:12, 14, 16

The way of deliverance will be through exile; this will finally teach the nation to forsake compromise with paganism.

Chapter 28 in Ezekiel has been an important chapter in historical interpretation on the subject of Satan. It parallels Isaiah 14, though in this case the king in the Ezekiel historical context is the king of Tyre, not Babylon. I quote the text here which is entitled a lament concerning the king of Tyre.

> You were the seal of perfection, full of wisdom and perfect in beauty. You were in Eden, the garden of God; every precious stone adorned you: carnelian, chrysolite and emerald, topaz, onyx and jasper, lapis lazuli, turquoise and beryl. Your settings and mountings were made of gold; on the day you were created they were prepared. You were anointed as a guardian cherub, for so I ordained you. You were on the holy mount of God; you walked among the fiery stones. You were blameless in your ways from the day you were created till wickedness was found in you. Through your widespread trade you were filled with violence, and you sinned. So I drove you in disgrace from the mount of God, and I expelled you, guardian cherub, from among the fiery stones. Your heart became proud on account of your beauty, and you corrupted your wisdom because of your splendor. So I threw you to the earth; I made a spectacle of you before kings. By your many sins and dishonest trade you have desecrated your sanctuaries.
>
> —EZEKIEL 28:12–18

Some parts of this do refer to the king of Tyre, especially the verses speaking of dishonest trade or the trade filling him with violence. Yet again, as in the Isaiah text, is this king described with the backdrop of a fallen angel? Satan himself? The verse that states that he was anointed as a guardian cherub ordained by God certainly does not literally fit the king of Tyre. In addition, it could not be said he was full of wisdom, perfect in beauty, and in the garden of Eden. Is this language only metaphor for the king of Tyre or something more?

We do not have absolute proof that this text is giving us information about Satan or Lucifer, but it fits the Book of Revelation text on the fall of Satan. This is indeed a very important text for how Christians have traditionally understood the fall of Satan.

Ezekiel 38 and 39 depict the final battles against Israel and the utter defeat of the nations that invade Israel though the powerful intervention of God. We are not told of the level of angelic power involved nor what the people of God are doing to win these most intense and final battles. In one picture the invading armies slay one another. In another picture they die by the direct intervention of God.

THE EXILIC PROPHET, THE BOOK OF DANIEL

The Book of Daniel provides us with content that has been very important to many who engaged in spiritual warfare. Daniel 9 has been very frequently quoted. The chapter quotes an intercessory prayer in which Daniel confesses the sins of Israel. He is in sackcloth and ashes as he represents himself as part of Israel and says, "We have sinned" (v. 5). This text is used to defend the concept of "representative repentance." Daniel acknowledges that the curses of the covenant of Mosaic Covenant have fallen upon the nation. However, in this great prayer he asks for God to fulfill His prophetic word from Jeremiah, that the desolation of Jerusalem would last seventy years.

The text is very clear. **Intercessory prayer is important in spiritual warfare whereby God's purposes are fulfilled. Though there is prophecy, God raises up an intercessor to partner with Him to bring about the fulfillment of His word.** While Daniel is praying the angel Gabriel appears to him. He is described as a man. Chapter 8 had previously introduced Gabriel. In that vision, Daniel hears a holy one speaking and another one asking how long it will take for the vision of that chapter to be fulfilled. Then a voice tells Gabriel to tell Daniel the meaning of the vision. Daniel says that he was terrified and fell prostrate on his face and into a deep sleep. But the angel touched him and raised him to his feet and told him what would happen in a later time of wrath. Following this experience Daniel says he was exhausted and lay ill for several days (this can mean that he was just very weak).

In chapter 9 Gabriel comes to Daniel at the time of the evening sacrifice. He came to give Daniel understanding: "I have now come to give you insight and understanding" (v. 22). Then he states, "As soon as you began to pray, an answer was given, which I have come to tell you, for you are highly esteemed" (v. 23).

This leads to the famous vision of the seventy weeks, usually interpreted as weeks of years which takes us to the time of the ministry of Yeshua, Jesus.

In chapter 10, we find that Daniel is again praying and fasting in a state of mourning for three weeks. As he stood by the bank of the Tigris river, he looked up and saw a man dressed in linen with "a belt of the fine gold from Uphaz around his waist. His body was like topaz, his face like lightning, his eyes like flaming torches, his arms and legs like the gleam of burnished bronze, and his voice like the sound of a multitude" (vv. 5–6). This figure reminds us of the vision of Yeshua in Revelation 1:12–16. Again Daniel falls into a deep sleep.

We are then told that Daniel's prayer was heard from the beginning. He was seeking God to understand a revelation of a great war. The messenger had come in response to Daniel's prayer. However, "The prince of the Persian kingdom resisted me twenty-one days. Then Michael, one of the chief princes, came to help me, because I was detained there with the king of Persia" (v. 13). Daniel became speechless before the angel, but he touched his lips and Daniel was able to speak.

The angel says,

> Do you know why I have come to you? Soon I will return to fight the prince of Persia, and when I go, the prince of Greece will come, but first I will tell you what is written the Book of Truth. (No one supports me against them except Michael, your prince. And in the first year of Darius the Mede, I took my stand to support and protect him.)
> —DANIEL 10:20–21; 11:1

After this a large section of prophecy is given concerning kings of the north (the Seleucids in the area of greater Syria) and the south (the Ptolemys of Egypt). Chapter 12:1 states, "At that time Michael, the great prince who protects your people, will arise. There will be a time of distress such as has not happened from the beginning of nations until then."

Then in verse 5 Daniel saw two others on the banks of the river on opposite sides. One of them said to the man clothed in linen who had been speaking to Daniel, who was above the waters, "How long will it be before these astonishing things are fulfilled" (v. 6). He was answered by the man clothed in linen, who was above the waters. Daniel was told to go his way until the end.

There is important information in these texts. Scholars agree that the Book of Daniel was very influential in second temple Judaism and established a consensus of beliefs among those who accepted the inspiration and authority of the Book of Daniel. This included the importance of angelic messengers. In addition, in some way angelic messengers engage in battles with evil beings that are princes over nations. This is the sense of the battle of Gabriel with the prince of Persia. He was hindered by this prince and unable to bring the answer to Daniel until Michael came and helped him.

This leaves us with several questions.

First, how is it that princes over unredeemed nations have spiritual power to withstand God's angels? We do not know how this is possible, but it is asserted here. Thus the text shows us a kind of spiritual warfare between angelic beings and other beings that are connected to unredeemed nations.

Secondly, is it possible that the prayers of Daniel are a part of the spiritual warfare that brings Michael to aid Gabriel so that the answer was brought to him? The text does not clearly say this. However, it does seem that Daniel's involvement is part of the spiritual warfare.

Does the text indicate that unredeemed nations have evil spiritual beings over those nations? They must be evil if they are resisting God's messengers. Do all nations, or peoples have connection to such beings? This would fit the very ideas in pagan societies and especially in the ancient Near East where there is a chief god over a nation or tribe.

When we think of pagan practices such as child sacrifices and other terrible practices to gain the favor of such gods, we have evidence that would cohere with the idea that pagan gods can be real beings of evil and not just imaginary beings. **So the whole idea of territorial spirits connected to people finds some basis on these texts.** Those who engage in spiritual warfare in the charismatic world believe this idea of territorial spirits is very important. It is taught that they hinder the spread of the Gospel. They have to be weakened or defeated by prayer, fasting, and by sometimes addressing these spirits. This teaching is very possibly correct but cannot be clearly proven by these texts. Prayer and fasting does have an effect in bringing about God's will, and it would be reasonable to hold that this has an effect on the dark spirits that are over nations.

Who is the figure of Michael? Some hold that Michael is a chief angel or perhaps the chief angel who is the guardian angel of the nation of Israel. However some have argued that Michael is Yeshua, Jesus, before His incarnation. This is a speculation, but not uncommon. The consensus of historical interpretation is that Michael is not Yeshua or Messiah pre-incarnate.

There is no evidence in Daniel of engaging in spiritual warfare by addressing evil spirits. Daniel simply did not do this. This practice has to be based on other texts or on prophetic revelation beyond the biblical texts.

We should note that there is much more information in the New Covenant Scriptures on prayer and spiritual warfare.

The Post Exilic Prophets

The Book of Zechariah

Zechariah provides new and important content on the themes of this book. Zechariah describes a vision in the second year of the Persian King Darius. The vision was of a man riding a red horse standing among the myrtle trees in a ravine. "Behind him were red, brown and white horses" (v. 8).

He then asks, "What are these, my lord?" (v. 9). We are told that there was **an angel talking with him**. Then we read that the man among the myrtle trees spoke. (This text is a bit confusing—is an angel interpreting the rest of the vision outside of the vision to Zechariah or is the angel within the vision interpreting it?) He says that the horses were "the ones the LORD sent to go throughout the earth" (v. 10). They reported to the angel among the myrtle trees and "found the whole world at rest and in peace" (v. 11).

The Angel of the Lord then asked, "LORD Almighty, how long will you withhold mercy from Jerusalem and the towns of Judah, which you have been angry with these seventy years. So the LORD spoke kind and comforting words to the angel who talked" to Zechariah (vv. 12–13). The LORD of course represents the name of God, YHWH.

The text continues to show a revelatory angel in another vision of four horns and four craftsmen in verses 18–20. Four craftsmen are described as throwing down the horns that came against Judah. The horns are the strength of the nations that oppressed Judah. Were these craftsman angels involved in overthrowing the nations, or is this only a visionary symbol? We are not told.

In chapter 2 there is another vision with a man with a measuring line. He is asked what he is going to do and says he will measure Jerusalem. However, the angel who was speaking to Zechariah is also present in this vision but then leaves and another angel comes to meet the first angel and tells him that Jerusalem will be a city without walls for the numerous people and livestock. "'For I,' says the LORD, 'will be a wall of fire around her, and I will be the glory in her midst'" (v. 5, NKJV).

The point is that angelic messengers here seem to be within visions but also perhaps beyond visions in the actual direct experiences of the prophet. Angels thus play an important role in the early chapters of this book.

Chapter 3 is one of the more important sections for the subject of this book. In this vision, Zechariah sees Joshua the high priest. The reader should note that this is the same basic name as Yeshua. Bible students for centuries have noted the parallels between Joshua the high priest and Yeshua as our ultimate High Priest. Joshua is part of a symbolic act where he is both high priest and ruler. At this next point we are not paralleling the life of Yeshua (Jesus). The Angel of the LORD and Satan are both standing before Joshua. Satan is at "standing at his right side to accuse him" (v. 1). The angel says, "The LORD rebuke you Satan! The LORD, who has chosen Jerusalem, rebuke you! Is not this man a burning stick snatched from the fire?" (v. 2). It is interesting to note here that **the angel does not himself rebuke Satan but speaks a prayer**: "The LORD rebuke you," which may have the force of "may the LORD rebuke you."

In this vision Joshua stands before the angel in filthy clothes, but the angel says to those standing before him to take off these clothes. He then says to Joshua, "I have taken away your sin" (v. 4). (Many identify the Angel of the LORD as pre-incarnate Messiah, Yeshua, Jesus.) Then the prophet Zechariah says, "Put a clean turban on his head" (v. 5). This was done. The Angel of the Lord then gives a charge to Joshua to walk in God's ways and that if he does so, he will govern his house.

Then we find that Joshua is symbolic of things to come and that God is going to bring His servant the branch (Isaiah 11 as well). This is connected to removing the sin of the land in a day.

In chapter 4 the angel who was speaking to him previously awakens him and gives him the vision of a lampstand with a bowl on top and seven lights on it. The vision includes two olive trees providing the oil to the lamps. The two olive trees providing the oil are Zerubbabel and Joshua who were appointed to serve the Lord, the one the civil governor and the other, as we have noted above, the high priest.

The visions continue into chapters 5 and 6. Chapter 5 presents the visions of a flying scroll and a woman in a basket. Again the angel is involved in dialogue with Zechariah and conveys the Word of God in interpreting the vision. In the vision of the woman in the basket, two women with wings like a stork lift the basket and take it to Babylonia. In chapter 6 the vision is of four chariots coming between two mountains of bronze. There are four different colored horses. Zechariah asks the angel who they are. The angel tells him that they are the four spirits of heaven. (Do they represent angels as well?)

These chapters of Zechariah are the most extensive in the Hebrew Bible where an angel is represented as the bearer of revelation. This pattern, as we saw, is found the Book of Daniel as well. The later chapters of Zechariah only say that the Word of the Lord came to the prophet. Angelic mediation is absent.

We do not read of angelic rulers in Zechariah but of angelic messengers. It seems clear that revelation can come from the Spirit of God directly, from the appearance of the Angel of the LORD who is a divine figure, or from a lesser angel.

The closing chapters of Zechariah depict the final battles over Israel, good and evil, and the invasion of the Holy Land. These huge battles are decided by the intervention of God and by supernatural anointing to fight. As we read in chapter 12, finally by the coming of the Holy One whose feet stand on the mount of Olives and His fight against these forces of evil. They are totally defeated. However, nothing is said about what the people of God do in Chapter 14 to attain the victory. However, this must be spiritual warfare at its climatic level of intensity and ultimate victory.

Excursus

C. Peter Wagner and F. Douglas Pennoyer, *Wrestling with Dark Angels*

As I mentioned before, C. Peter Wagner was one of the most important professors of missions in the last half of the twentieth century and taught at Fuller Theological Seminary in Pasadena, California. F. Douglas Pennoyer is the son of missionaries to the Philippines and is the dean of Cook School of Intercultural Studies at Biola University in La Mirada, California. These are some examples from their book of territorial powers of darkness.

> **Uruguay-Brazil Border:** Individuals who were closed to the Gospel on the Uruguay side of the

town's main street, became open when they crossed over to the Brazilian side.

Costa Rica: Symptoms of mental illness left a patient when she traveled to the United States; they reappeared when she returned to Costa Rica. Christian psychologist Rita Cabezas was told by one of the demons that they were limited to their territory and could not go to the U. S.

Navajo reservation: Herman Williams, a Navajo Alliance pastor, suffered serious physical symptoms which left as he crossed the reservation boundary for treatment in the city, and recurred when he entered the reservation. The spirits causing this were traced to a witch doctor whom they later killed....

Argentina: Omar Cabrera, though prayer and fasting exercises a regular ministry of identifying the spirits controlling certain cities, breaks their power, and finds little subsequent resistance to god's power for salvation and healing....

Argentina: Edgardo Silvoso reports the accelerated multiplication of churches within a radius of 100 miles of the city of Rosario after a team broke the power of the spirit of Merigildo in 1985.

C. Peter Wagner and F. Douglas Pennoyer, eds., *Wrestling with Dark Angels,* (Ventura, CA: Regal Books, 1990), 81–82.

Derek Prince, *Blessing or Curse: You Can Choose*

Derek Prince was one of the most noted international teachers in the charismatic world of the last generation. His defense of the ministry of deliverance, fivefold ministry restoration, and the power of God were world renowned. In this book he argues that one of the keys to spiritual warfare is to remove curses that are upon individuals, families, tribes, and whole nations due to actions that bring a curse according to the Bible. Sometimes the believers have to intercede, repent, and seek to bring a change in their nation and thereby have the curse removed. This section is from his chapter on anti-Semitism.

About four thousand years ago God made a choice that has affected all subsequent history. He was looking for a man who would meet His conditions so that he might ultimately become a channel of God's blessing to all nations. The man he chose was called Abram (later renamed Abraham). God's purpose in choosing Abraham is unfolded in Genesis 12:2–3. Characteristically, blessing and curse are closely connected. God pronounces four promises of blessing upon Abraham: "I will bless you." "You shall be a blessing." "I will bless those who bless you." "In you all the families of the earth shall be blessed." Imposed in the midst of these blessings is a curse. "I will curse him who curses you." Taken together, these Scriptures [Numbers 24] make it clear that both the blessing and the curse originally pronounced on Abraham were extended to his descendants, Isaac and Jacob, and then on to their succeeding generations, who are today known collectively as the Jewish people.

God did not make it impossible for His enemies to curse Abraham, Isaac, Jacob and their descendants, but He did ensure that no one could do it with impunity. From that time onward, no one has ever cursed the Jewish people without bringing upon himself a far more fearful curse; that of almighty God. In contemporary speech, the attitude that provokes this curse of God is summed up in a single word: anti-Semitism.

It would take a full-length book to trace the out-working of this course in the history of individuals and nations from the time of the patriarchs until our day. Suffice it to say that in nearly 4,000 years, no individual and no nation has ever cursed the Jewish people without bringing upon themselves in return the blighting curse of God....

Here is one main reason for the present lukewarm, powerless condition of so much of Christendom—especially in Europe and the Middle East, where anti-Semitism is most deeply entrenched. . . the solution: open acknowledgement of anti-Semitism as a sin, followed by repentance and renunciation. This will result in a deep, inner change of heart toward the Jewish people, and a recognition of the measureless spiritual blessings the Christian Church has received through them.

Excerpts from *Blessing or Curse* by Derek Prince, copyright © 1990. Used by permission of Chosen, a division of Baker Publishing Group.

SUMMARY OF THE HEBREW BIBLE

THE STUDY OF the Hebrew Bible provides a limited amount of information on the issue of angels, demons, and spiritual warfare. The Bible to this point is very restrained.

The matters of spiritual warfare are depicted in the contests of Moses with Aaron and the magicians of Egypt. There is obvious supernatural power operating through the magicians, but God's power is superior. Hence the gods of Egypt are vanquished in the Exodus. The Bible does not give us clear information as to what these gods are and do, but there is an assumed knowledge of paganism. Israel's victory is through the prophetic leadership of Moses under God's direction.

Israel is charged to conquer the land of Canaan. She is not told to bring deliverance to the pagan peoples whereby they can become free of the power of pagan gods. She is to wipe out the whole culture. This is the nature of Israel's assigned spiritual warfare. Israel is to be completely apart from the contamination of pagan gods by simply eliminating the people within her borders that are given to the horrendous practices that were part of worshipping those gods. Israel is not to conquer the nations outside her borders by such means. Rather, she is to be a light to the nations from within her cleansed or purified land. Israel is to be free from demonic power by simply living in a way that has nothing to do with these powers and by living in a land where there is no practice of idolatry and occult magic.

The Book of Samuel reveals an evil spirit that comes upon Saul that motivates him to seek to kill David. This is a glimpse of an evil realm but with little depth of information.

The historical books mostly speak of spiritual warfare in terms of the actual literal battles that Israel must wage against other nations that are under other gods. Do these gods have power or is their reality an illusion? One could look at different passages as supporting either conclusion, but the evidence as a whole leads us to the conclusion that at least some of these gods have power and that it is an evil power to be avoided. There is the indication in both Isaiah and Ezekiel that there is a chief power of evil associated with a fall from God's heavenly throne, and this is spoken of in terms of the analogy with the king of Babylon and the king of Tyre. In the context of the gods with Elijah, the gods are silent. This parallels many stories from the mission field where the powers of darkness are simply shut down before the prayers of the missionaries.

The books of Daniel and Zechariah reveal more about angels, and we find angels acting as messengers of revelation in both books. This is distinct from the Angel of God figure, again in our view the pre-incarnate Messiah. We are given two names for angels in Daniel: Michael and Gabriel. We do see the picture in Daniel of a dark prince over Persia resisting Gabriel and Michael as they came to his aid. So there is something represented here as war in the heavenlies.

In conclusion, the Hebrew Bible does not say very much about angels or demonic powers. It emphasizes the charge to Israel to live apart from idolatry and all occult involvement. It recognizes that there is such dark power but does not answer to curiosity. Israel's answer to dark powers is to live purely in her own land, to not permit idolaters or practitioners of the occult to live, and thus to maintain the purity of the land. Thereby Israel would be a light to the nations. Israel did not follow these directions, so there was a degree of corporate contamination that was greater or lesser during different periods of Israel's history.

This is a book about what the Bible says. We should note that there is a significant amount of literature, for example, the inter-testamental literature, that presents much more representations of the powers of both angels and demonic powers. This is spiritual literature written by Jews between the end of the writings of the Hebrew Bible and the New Covenant period. These texts cannot be looked at as Scripture and were not accepted as such in first century Judaism or Christianity. However, they are a context for cultural backgrounds or for the ideas that many believed just before the coming of Yeshua.

PART II

ANGELS, DEMONS, AND
SPIRITUAL WARFARE IN THE
NEW COVENANT SCRIPTURES

Introduction

THE NEW COVENANT AND THE HEBREW BIBLE

T HE CONTRAST BETWEEN the New Covenant Scriptures and the Hebrew Bible is quite marked. The subject of angels, demons, and spiritual warfare—except for literal wars with nations or peoples—is underplayed in the Hebrew Bible. It is as if we are looking at an old black and white movie that has not been well preserved. In the New Covenant Scriptures, it is as if we are looking at a well-defined color movie, at least on some of these matters. The New Covenant is not completely clear on the issue of how to do spiritual warfare against the more powerful princes of darkness. However, it shows that there is one great evil power called Satan or the Accuser. It also shows that there are demons that inhabit or attach to people who can make them mentally unstable, physically sick, and can influence them to evil behavior. They can even trap or bind them in patterns of evil. It also shows such powers ruling over human communities. The descriptions of ministry to people in demonic bondage is much more extensive.

Chapter 5

ANGELS, DEMONS, AND SPIRITUAL WARFARE IN THE GOSPELS

THE SYNOPTIC GOSPELS (THE FIRST THREE GOSPELS)

The birth narratives

Angelic involvement in the birth narratives of Matthew and Luke are significant. In Matthew, the much shorter account, after Miriam (Mary) was found with a child, an angel of the Lord appeared to Joseph in a dream and said, "Joseph, son of David, do not be afraid to take Mary home as your wife, because what is conceived in her is from the Holy Spirit" (Matt. 1:20). When Joseph woke up, he did what the angel of the Lord had commanded him. I want us to take note of the assumption of the text that Joseph responded on the basis that he could discern an angelic vision in a dream as trustworthy, giving him true information. Again, we see the pattern we saw in Daniel and Zechariah that angels (a word actually meaning messenger in Hebrew) communicate information from God.

Again, the angel appears to Joseph in a dream and tells him to escape with Miriam and the infant child Yeshua to Egypt. After King Herod died, the angel again appeared to Joseph in a dream and commanded him to go back to the land of Israel. Having been warned in another dream, he settled in Nazareth.

The stories in Luke provide more information on angelic involvement. In Luke 1:11–25, we read about the angelic encounter with Zechariah the priest. Zechariah was on duty to burn incense, an angel of the Lord appeared to him at the side of the altar of incense. He was gripped with fear. The angel tells him to not fear, but that his wife Elizabeth will bear a son and he is to call him John. The angel also describes the nature of John's ministry.

Zechariah is able to dialogue with the angel and asks how he can be sure of the fulfillment of the promise. The angel now tells him that his name is Gabriel, the same angel that appeared to Daniel. He will be dumb because he did not believe. This is a supernatural act to confirm the certainty of the promise.

In verses 26–38 of Luke we read of the angel Gabriel and his interaction with Mary. He went to Nazareth and appeared to Miriam (Mary). She was given the prophecy that she will become pregnant by the Holy Spirit without any sexual involvement with her husband. The promise of inheriting David's throne was declared. She is given further information on her cousin Elizabeth and her pregnancy. These passages are very Jewish in the poetic expressions of Zechariah and Miriam. They have the mark of authenticity.

In Luke chapter 2 we read of an angel of the Lord appearing to shepherds living in the fields with their flocks. An angel of the Lord appeared to them and the glory of the Lord shone around them. They were terrified. The angel announces the birth of the Messiah and a description of what they will see when they find Him. In verse 13 we read something new—a great company of the heavenly host appeared with the angel, praising God. This is described as a "heavenly host" of angels. Then the angels left them, and the shepherds went to Bethlehem to find the child.

The temptations in the wilderness

The first three Gospels all present the account of Yeshua being tested (tempted) in the wilderness by Satan. Mark's account is very brief (1:12–13). The Holy Spirit is the one who led Him to the wilderness for this test. The forty days in the desert is more clearly connected to Israel's forty years in the desert.

Matthew presents His temptation as coming at the end of a forty day fast when He was hungry. The first temptation is to act outside of the will of God for provision: "If you are the Son of God, tell these stones to become bread" (4:3). This was to demonstrate his power over natural law. Then came the test of power over death before the people by doing the great miracle of throwing Himself down from the highest point of the temple: "If you are the Son of God,...throw yourself down" (v. 6). And the third temptation was to attain universal rule by bowing down and worshiping Satan:

> Again, the devil took him up on a very high mountain and showed him all the kingdoms of the world and their splendor. "All this I will give you," he said, "if you will bow down and worship me."
>
> —MATTHEW 4:8–9

In each case Yeshua resists the devil by quoting the Word of God.

Yeshua's response to the devil is a model for many on how to engage the spiritual warfare of resisting the devil. **Standing on the basis of the Word of God, knowing this Word and quoting it against the demonic powers**

is a foundation for spiritual warfare. The Lukan account provides the same basic content in chapter 4:1–13. It adds the statement that the devil left Him until an opportune time (v. 13). We therefore know that this was not the only time of testing. Matthew adds that after the devil left Him: "angels came and attended him" (v. 11). In verse 10 of the Matthew account Yeshua directly addresses the devil and says, "Away from me, Satan."

Can we follow the example of Yeshua and sometimes directly address Satan? This is a source of great debate. We do not have examples in the New Testament of others addressing Satan himself and commanding him, but we do have examples of addressing demons who inhabit or are attached to people.

We also note from these passages that the angels came to attend Yeshua. Angels do more than just convey messages, and we will present New Covenant teaching that shows that angels have larger roles.

Beginning from Matthew 4:23, Mark 1:21, and Luke 4:31, the ministry of Yeshua is characterized by healing the sick and casting out demons. Sometimes the sickness is demonic, but the text presents other healings that are not connected to casting out demons.

It is not beneficial for our purpose to exhaustively present all the passages that deal with deliverance ministry or the casting out of demons. Rather, it is important that we present a sufficient number of passages to give the broad sweep of how deliverance ministry is presented.

In Luke 4:33–37 we read the account of a deliverance that took place on the Sabbath.

> A man possessed by a demon, an impure spirit…cried out at the top of his voice, "Go away!

What do you want with us, Jesus of Nazareth? Have you come to destroy us? I know who you are—the Holy One of God." "Be quiet!" Jesus said sternly, "Come out of him." Then the demon threw the man down before them all and came out without injuring him. All the people were amazed and said to each other, "What words these are! With authority and power he gives orders to evil spirits and they come out!" And the news about him spread throughout the surrounding area.

The account in Mark (1:21–28) does not add significant information to the account we referenced. In Matthew 8:16 the text informs us that he "drove out the spirits with a word."

There was a limited practice of deliverance in the Jewish community during the first century. The people knew what demon spirits were, but nothing prepared them for the authority of Yeshua in speaking a word and casting out evil spirits. Indeed, there is nothing like this in the Jewish literature of that era. This level of power and authority was something new and a powerful accreditation of the ministry of Yeshua.

Herein is new information added what was presented in the Hebrew Bible. One is that the demons can speak through the person they oppress or inhabit. The other is that they at least may have significant immediate knowledge. The demon in this account immediately perceives who Yeshua is, maybe by perceiving the awesome power of anointing that was present. This will be repeated again and again.

Mark 5:1–20 presents the case of a man who was severely demon possessed. The parallels are in Luke 8:26–38 and in Matthew 8:28–31. Matthew tells us that there were two demon possessed men living in a cemetery. Mark and Luke emphasize one, probably the one who after the deliverance begged to go with Yeshua. As he was charged to proclaim what the Lord had done for him, perhaps he was a known person to the early followers of Yeshua. We will concentrate on the Luke and Mark accounts.

The effect of demon possession appears to be very like medical insanity. We read, "For a long time this man had not worn clothes or lived in a house, but had lived in the tombs" (Luke 8:27). Mark tells us that the man with the evil spirit came to meet Him. He could not be bound even with chains on his hands and feet. We recognize here the assertion of a supernatural power. "Night and day...he would cry out and cut himself with stones" (Mark 5:5). This is a very pathetic picture.

When he saw Yeshua from a distance, he ran and fell on his knees and shouted at the top of his voice, "What do you want with me, Jesus, Son of the Most High God? In God's name don't torture me" (v. 7). Jesus had commanded the evil spirit to come out of him.

Again, we find that the evil spirit has supernatural knowledge. When Yeshua asked for his name, he said, "My name is Legion: for we are many" (v. 9, KJV). This shows that it is possible for many demons to be attached to or inhabit one human being. We cannot comprehend this in our normal material and special categories.

The demon, probably the leader of the legion, begs Yeshua to not send them out of the area. They asked to be allowed to inhabit a herd of pigs. Yeshua gave permission, but the solution of the demon was short lived since the pigs were somehow spooked (a pretty accurate word for what happened) and ran off a steep bank into the lake and drowned.

All of this aroused the interest of the people of the town who came out to see what happened. In amazement they saw the formerly possessed man being in his right mind and clothed. They were afraid. The people were told what happened by those who witnessed it, including the account of the pigs, and they plead with Yeshua to leave. Raising pigs is an indication that this was not a Jewish area.

We learn a lot from this account. The demons are commanded to leave. The demons can converse through the oppressed individual, though Yeshua, in His ministry, does not usually converse with the demons. In this case, it seems that the leader of the legion converses. The demons can inhabit animals as well as human beings. Finally, demons can cause manifestations that are like severe mental illness. We are not told what demons are, whether fallen angels or some other kind of being.

The practice of deliverance ministers in asking for the demon to identify himself or themselves by name is largely derived from this passage. There is a teaching that knowing the name of the demon gives the minister greater power in effecting the deliverance. Others believe that one should not ask for a name but should know this through prophetic discernment and the symptoms of the person being served in prayer ministry.

In Matthew 9:32 Yeshua cast a demon out of a man who could not talk. The response of the crowd again indicates the unusual level of immediate authority.

> The crowd was amazed and said, "Nothing like this has ever been seen in Israel." But the Pharisees said, "It is by the prince of demons that he drives out demons."
>
> —MATTHEW 9:33–34

We will address this response in a later section.

Sending out the disciples and the seventy-two

In Mark 6:6–13, Matthew 10:6–15 and Luke 9:1–9, Yeshua sends out the twelve disciples. They are charged to heal the sick and were given authority to drive out demons. In Mark we read, "They drove out many demons and anointed many sick people with oil and healed them" (6:13). Healing sicknesses and driving out demons are distinguished but overlapping since a demon can cause the sickness. The Luke account uses the term "cure diseases" (9:1).

I prefer to emphasize the account of the sending of the seventy-two in Luke 10:1–24. Yeshua sends the disciples and tells them that if they are welcome in a town they are to, "Heal the sick there and say to them, 'The kingdom of God has come near to you'" (v. 9). When the seventy-two returned with joy they said, "Lord, even the demons submit to us in your name" (v. 17). Yeshua responds with an important statement,

> I saw Satan fall like lightning from heaven. I have given you authority to trample on snakes and scorpions and to overcome all the power of the enemy; nothing will harm you. However, do not rejoice that the spirits submit to you, but rejoice that your names are written in heaven.
> —Luke 10:18

The disciples recognize that their experience of the described level authority and power to cast demons, and their submission to them, was without parallel. They were amazed. Yeshua counsels them to not rejoice in this, but that their names are written in heaven. However, before this statement, Yeshua states that something enormous had happened through the ministry of the seventy-two. Yeshua had been able to cast out demons with a word, but the transferring of this power meant that His expanding movement would have unlimited power to free people in bondage to demonic power. He describes it in these terms, "Behold, I give you the authority to trample on serpents and scorpions, and over all the power of the enemy, and nothing shall by any means hurt you" (Luke 10:18, NKJV).

I think this passage is very important for spiritual warfare. The meaning of Satan falling from heaven is highly charged symbolic language, and we cannot know the exact literal content for interpretation. However, falling from heaven means losing authority. **So the defeat of Satan is through delivering people from satanic power through the ministry of deliverance, healing, and the proclamation of the good news of the kingdom. This is not the only means of spiritual warfare but is central in the Gospels.**

The accusation of Yeshua working by the power of Satan

In Matthew 12:22–37 and Luke 11:14–28 we have the parallel accounts of Yeshua being accused of driving out demons by the power of Satan, or Beelzebub, the prince of demons. Beelzebub means Lord of flies. The context was Yeshua's ministry to a blind and mute man. Yeshua healed him so that he could talk and see. We are not told how much of the problem was demonic, but the text seems to indicate a connection to the demonization and the physical problems.

Yeshua's response is again very important. He states,

> Every kingdom divided against itself will be ruined,
> and every city or household divided against itself

> will not stand. If Satan drives out Satan, he is divided against himself. How then can his kingdom stand? And if I drive out demons by Beelzebub, by whom do your people drive them out? So then they will be your judges. But if it is by the Spirit of God that I drive out demons, then the kingdom of God has come upon you.
>
> —MATTHEW 12:25–28

This is very important content. Both Yeshua and His opponents in this passage agree that Satan or the devil leads a kingdom of evil spirits. However, Satan would not be in the business of releasing people from demonic bondage or he would be destroying his own kingdom. Yeshua accepts that there is deliverance ministry in the Jewish community; but as the literature of the time shows, it was very limited and was not with anything like the authority and power of Yeshua and His disciples. Indeed, the driving out of demons with the authority and power that is demonstrated by Yeshua (and His disciples) **shows that the Kingdom of God has come upon them**, and that that Kingdom is defeating the kingdom of Satan.

Yeshua goes on to teach a parable. No one can enter a strong man's house and carry off his possessions unless he first ties up the strong man. Then he is able to rob his house. How is this strong man bound? Yeshua does not say. Some deliverance ministers take this verse to say that they should command leading demons when there is an oppressed person with multiple demons and say to the leading demon and the others, "I bind you in the name of Yeshua." They will use Matthew 18 for support for this. However, the text does not really prove this method. Rather it seems that Satan is bound by the very authority/power of the person of Yeshua and His action. In addition, this authority transfers to His disciples and they are able to command demons to leave. If there is authority to command demons, **then is there authority to command powers of darkness over territories?** This is a great point of controversy today and shall be addressed after more passages are reviewed.

Satan steals the seed of the message of the Gospel

In this text (Matthew 13:19 and Mark 4:15) concerning the parable of the four soils and the sower, the seed that falls on the wayside and does not spring up at all is said to be stolen by Satan so that the potential listener does not grasp the preaching of the Gospel at all. Some people are under such satanic influence that the Gospel has no effect.

The devil sows bad seed

In Matthew 13:24–30, the Kingdom of heaven is compared to a man who sowed good seed in his field but an enemy came and sowed weeds among the wheat. In verse 39 we read that the enemy that sowed the bad seed is the devil.

So in this text the devil is active, sowing false information and bad seed that will grow up corrupting the garden. Yet both are to grow together in the world until harvest. So Satan has his messages, messengers, and his disciples!

The post-transfiguration deliverance of an epileptic boy

All three Synoptic Gospels present this narrative (Mark 9:14–29; Luke 9:37–44, and Matthew 17:14–21).

In the Mark account, verses 17 and 18, the father tells Yeshua about the condition of his son. He states,

> Teacher, I brought you my son, who is possessed by a spirit that has robbed him of speech. Whenever it seizes him, it throws him to the ground, he foams at the mouth, gnashes his teeth and becomes rigid. I

asked your disciples to drive out the spirit, but they could not.

Yeshua responds, "You unbelieving generation...how long shall I put up with you? Bring the boy to me" (v. 19). Then the text describes the situation with some detail worth quoting:

> So they brought him. When the spirit saw Jesus, it immediately threw the boy into a convulsion. He fell to the ground and rolled around, foaming at the mouth. Jesus asked the boy's father, "How long has he been like this?" "From childhood," he answered. "It has often thrown him into the fire or water to kill him. But if you can do anything, take pity on us and help us." "'If you can'?" said Jesus, "Everything is possible for one who believes." Immediately the boy's father exclaimed, "I do believe; help me overcome my unbelief!" When Jesus saw that a crowd was running to the scene, he rebuked the impure spirit, "You deaf and mute spirit," he said, "I command you, come out of him and never enter him again." The spirit shrieked, convulsed him violently and came out. The boy looked so much like a corpse that many said, "He's dead." But Jesus took him by the hand and lifted him to his feet, and he stood up. After Jesus had gone indoors, his disciples asked him privately, "Why couldn't we drive it out.?" He replied, "This kind can come out only by prayer."
>
> —Mark 9:20–29

Other manuscripts add fasting to prayer.

In the Matthew account we are given more information on the answer to the disciple's question.

He replied, "Because you have so little faith. Truly I tell you, if you have faith as small as a mustard seed, you can say to this mountain, 'Move from here to there,' and it will move. Nothing will be impossible for you."

—MATTHEW 17:20

Spiritual warfare and deliverance ministries have taken directions from this text, but often with interpretations whose certainty is doubtful.

First, when Yeshua responds to the situation and says that the generation is faithless or unbelieving, some think He refers to the disciples. However, He is speaking to the whole generation. It is possible that the power of unbelief worked against the disciples and their level of faith for this situation was not great enough. In Nazareth we read that Yeshua could not do His ordinary supernatural ministry due to the unbelief of the town (Matt. 13:58). Apparently a spiritual atmosphere of unbelief can be established that hinders the power of the supernatural in bringing healing and deliverance. It is likely that Yeshua is addressing the people who, in seeing the terrible situation, responded as if nothing could be done, though the reputation of Yeshua and His disciples by this time was widespread.

Some have thought that the statement on prayer (and fasting in some manuscripts) was directed toward spending time in prayer and fasting before engaging in such ministry. It is probably wise council to do so. Prayer and fasting is a way to enter into higher levels of authority power by which a person can deal with more difficult situations.

Matthew points to the fact that the faith of the disciples was not sufficient for this, though they had had the wonderful experience of Luke 9 and 10. Whether the situation of unbelief was with the disciples or with the unbelieving crowd, it was too much for them. Yeshua notes that faith as a mustard seed can move mountains. I understand this to be saying that to move in authority and power one must develop one's faith/authority/power through the practice of prayer and fasting. So Yeshua is calling His disciples to a deeper life of prayer. It is not just about prayer preparation before an actual deliverance session.

In Mark 9:38–41 we read the account of the disciples' offense at someone driving out demons in the name of Yeshua though he was not part of the band that was following Yeshua. They told him to stop, but Yeshua said that they should not stop him, for one who does miracles in His name will not be able to say anything bad against Yeshua and His disciples. Apparently Yeshua accepted that one was able to do this work on the basis of connecting in faith to Him, even if not part of the band of disciples.

Binding and loosing

At first glance it would seem that Matthew 18:15–20 is not a passage about spiritual warfare, but one about congregational discipline. The passage tells us how to deal with a fellow Yeshua believer who is in sin or sins against one of them. (There are different text traditions.) One is to go alone to confront the sin. The issue is not to be spread in gossip. If there is no repentance, then one is to take one or two others. They confront the issue together but will also be potential witnesses if there is no repentance. If there is no repentance, then they are to tell it to the congregation. Whether this is through elders or directly is not stated in the text. If the person will not listen to the congregation, then he is to be treated as a pagan or a tax collector that is no longer part of the fellowship. Enforcing standards in congregational life has spiritual warfare implications since by maintaining righteousness in the congregation the grounds for demonic oppression are diminished. The key verses that are thought to deal with spiritual warfare follow.

> Truly I tell you, whatever you bind on earth will be bound in heaven, and whatever you loose on earth will be loosed in heaven. Again, truly I tell you that if two of you on earth agree about anything they ask for, it will be done for them by my Father in heaven. For where two or three gather in my name, there am I with them.
>
> —MATTHEW 18:18–20

Proponents of spiritual warfare have used these verses to declare binding and loosing over individuals during deliverance ministry and over regions with regard to princes of darkness. The formula is as follows: "I bind (name of spirit or type of spirit or prince of darkness) and loose (the person or the territory or the people in the territory), from your power."

Some of the readers may be familiar with this formula in prayer meetings that seek to do spiritual warfare. However, the text is about the judicial authority of declaring a person to be no longer part of the community. The words *binding* and *loosing* were understood in first century Judaism as the judicial authority of the court of elders and ultimately the supreme court in Israel, the Sanhedrin. Binding is to declare behavior forbidden and loosing is to declare behavior permitted. In addition, binding penalties could be enjoined. Such authority was called "the keys" and was spoken concerning Yeshua giving the keys of the kingdom of heaven to Peter and the apostles (in Matthew 16). Even the passage about two or three agreeing may be rooted in a judicial council of three (a *bet din*).

Yeshua goes beyond the court meaning and gives another application. He notes that when there is agreement in a prayer of two or three, it will be done by the Father. This has to be real faith agreement, a type of faith that comes from God and out of our relationship to Him. It is not just that any believers can just say words and have what they say. It is a depth of heart agreement born from God.

So there may be a secondary application in this text for spiritual warfare when believers pray to loose people from the power of the devil and even to loose regions from the powers of darkness. However, we still have to address the type of prayer or spiritual speaking that can be effective in extending the Kingdom of God and seeing the retreat of the kingdom of darkness.

The recognition of Satan's temptation through others

Yeshua recognizes that Satan (which can be a euphemism for demonic power) can inspire to evil in subtle ways. In Matthew 16:21–22, Mark 8:31–33, and Luke 9:21–22, Yeshua shares about His coming suffering, death, and resurrection. Peter took Him aside and said, "This shall never happen to you!" (Matt. 16:22).

Yeshua's response is not just to Peter, but to the enemy speaking through Peter. The temptation is to not go the way of the cross. He says, "Get behind me, Satan! You are a stumbling block to me; you do not have in mind the concerns of God, but merely the human concerns" (v. 23). One can therefore be tempted through people who give place to ideas that are from the enemy. One must be on guard and resist this.

The passage continues with the teaching of Yeshua that all His followers have to take up their crosses and follow Him.

Angels also figure in this passage, for Yeshua says He will come in His Father's glory with His angels and reward each person according to what He has done.

Satan enters into Judas who betrays Yeshua

Then Satan entered Judas called Iscariot, one of the Twelve. And Judas went to the chief priests and the officers of the temple guard and discussed with them how he might betray Jesus.

—LUKE 22:3-4

We are not told if this is through a sub demon under Satan's control or directly. The importance of Yeshua and His destiny would be worthy of Satan's direct involvement. Of course, the work of Satan does not totally supersede the will of the individual. The person has to give in to the temptation. There has been much speculation as to the motives of Satan. Indeed, some have thought he was trying to force Yeshua's hand and to get Him to finally overthrow the Romans and take over.

The warning to Peter and the disciples

"You will all fall away," Jesus told them, "for it is written, 'I will strike the shepherd, and the sheep will be scattered.'" ...Peter declared, "Even if all fall away, I will not." "Truly I tell you," Yeshua answered, "Today—yes, tonight—before the rooster crows twice you yourself will disown me three times."

—MARK 14:27-30

In the Luke version, Yeshua's prediction is preceded by these words,

> Simon, Simon, Satan has asked to sift all of you as wheat. But I have prayed for you, Simon, that your faith may not fail. And when you have turned back, strengthen your brothers.
>
> —Luke 22:31–32

We can easily see that Yeshua warning that the powers of darkness are involved in this situation. However, He encourages them that they will all come through it.

The temptation in the Garden of Gethsemane and in the Crucifixion

Many have taken the account of Yeshua's wrestling in prayer in the garden before His crucifixion as an intense spiritual war with the powers of darkness. Some have thought that the cup that Yeshua wanted God to take was the danger that He would die in the garden before fulfilling His destiny of death and resurrection. Others have thought that Yeshua was seeking to find a righteous way out of the crucifixion. Powers of darkness may be in mind when Yeshua's spoke to Peter and the disciples:

> "Simon," he said to Peter… "Could you not keep watch for one hour? Watch and pray so that you will not fall into temptation. The spirit is willing, but the body is weak."
>
> —Mark 14:37–38

In Luke 22:43 we read that an angel strengthened Yeshua in this trial in the garden. So it is clear that angels have power and can release energizing strength and encouragement.

At the arrest of Yeshua, He says to the elders and officers who had come to arrest Him, "But this is your hour—when the darkness reigns" (Luke 22:53). Context leads me to believe that we are talking about demonic power and not only the evil being chosen by the religious leaders.

At that time Matthew records that one of the twelve cut off the ear of one of the servants of the High priest. John tells us that it was Peter (John 18:10). In Matthew 26:52–53, Jesus says,

> "Put your sword back in its place...for all who draw the sword will die by the sword. Do you think I cannot call on my Father, and he will at once put at my disposal more than twelve legions of angels?"

In this interesting text, angels are represented in military terms; they can go forth as an army. We have noted other texts with this orientation from the Hebrew text; but here we see something of angels involved in war, both spiritual and perhaps physically.

In addition, it is not a stretch to perceive the powers of darkness involved in the Crucifixion, but the apparent victory of Satan was no victory at all.

Angels involved in the Resurrection

In the Resurrection accounts in the Gospels we find angelic involvement. In Matthew we read how with a violent earthquake an angel of the Lord rolled back the stone and sat upon it. The guards saw Him and were so afraid they shook and became like dead men. He is described as having an appearance like lightning and his clothes were as white as snow.

This angel appeared to the women who came to the tomb and told them to not be afraid. The angel announced the Resurrection, invited them to look into the tomb and to go and tell His disciples that He rose from the dead and would meet with them in Galilee.

In Mark the account is very similar. The women saw the angel in the tomb, sitting on the right side. He gives the same instruction.

In the Luke account two angels appear to the women. They are described as wearing clothes that were gleaming like lightning. Again, they announce the Resurrection and they quote Yeshua's prediction.

ANGELS, DEMONS, AND SPIRITUAL WARFARE IN THE GOSPEL OF JOHN

At the end of a very difficult passage due to the issue of who Yeshua is speaking to in text to text in John 8, we read: "To the Jews who had believed in him, Jesus said" (v. 31); and then in verse 44, Yeshua declares,

> You belong to your father, the devil, and you want to carry out your father's desire. He was a murderer from the beginning, not holding to the truth, for there is no truth in him. When he lies, he speaks his native language, for he is a liar and the father of lies.

Most Evangelical interpreters see this referring to a group of religious leaders that were present.

Some of the Jews, probably the religious leaders, say, "Aren't we right in saying that you are a Samaritan and demon-possessed?" (v. 48). Yeshua answered that He was not demon possessed but honored His Father.

The sense of these texts is that Yeshua is teaching that individuals and groups can be oriented toward evil, and that evil orientation can be fostered or further fixed by demonic power.

Satan enters into Judas

In John 13:26 Yeshua responds to the question of who will betray Him. Yeshua says, "It is the one to whom I will give this piece of bread when I have dipped it in the dish." When He gave it to Judas Iscariot, we read, "As soon as Judas took the bread, Satan entered into him" (v. 27).

The text there does not indicate that satanic influence or entering into a person is predetermined but that it reinforces a decision for evil. We see stages of influence, such as Peter's words denying that Yeshua would need to be crucified to the ultimate fixing of evil purpose through the devil.

In the account of the Resurrection in John, two angels appeared to Mary Magdalene. They were sitting where the body of Jesus was. The scene soon changes, and Jesus appears to the women. As in the synoptic Gospels, angels are involved in the Resurrection.

SUMMARY OF THE GOSPELS

We conclude from the Gospels that Yeshua taught and exemplified in His ministry that demons are real and can inhabit, oppress, and influence human beings. In severe situations, at least, these demons need to be driven out. More than one demon may be involved in the oppression. Preaching the Gospel and freeing people from demonic power in deliverance ministry is the primary means of spiritual warfare in the Gospels. We also noted that Satan or his demonic powers can influence individuals and groups of people including a leadership group. The world (human societies) is under the power of Satan and needs to be freed from his power.

EXCURSUS

Cindy Jacobs, *Possessing the Gates of the Enemy*

Cindy Jacobs is one of the most well-known charismatic spokespersons writing, speaking, and acting in the realm of spiritual warfare and intercession in the English-speaking world.

> Prayer walks are a form of corporate intercession that take the intercessors directly to the battlefield, usually a home or a neighborhood. John Dawson speaks of battling for your neighborhood through prayer walks in his book *Taking Our Cities for God.* John moved into an ethnic neighborhood in Los Angeles full of gang violence and drugs. He says,
>
> "Several years ago my staff and I went on a prayer walk around our neighborhood. We stood in front of every house, rebuked Satan's work in Jesus's name and prayed for a revelation of Jesus in the life of each family. We are still praying. There is a long way to God, but social, economic, and spiritual transformation is evident. There were times when demonic oppression almost crushed my soul. I received a death threat. My tires were slashed. I was often depressed at the sight of boarded-up houses, unemployed youth, and disintegrating families, but I was determined not to run away. Today there are at least nine Christian families in the block where I live, and there is a definite sense of the Lord's peace. The neighborhood is no longer disintegrating. People are renovating their houses, and

a sense of community is being established around the Christian families."

Prayer walks are being implemented across many nations. Graham Kendricks has had up to 150,000 people involved in marches in England. Some churches such as the Dwelling Place in Hemet, California, enter the Christmas parades in their cities to witness and pass out tracts. Joshua 1:3 says, "Every place that the sole of your foot will tread upon I have given you." In prayer walks you work to "take the land" for the Gospel or establish the borders of your city. As you walk you are taking back land from the enemy.

Except from *Possessing the Gates of the Enemy* by Cindy Jacobs, copyright © 1991. Used by permission of Chosen, a division of Baker Publishing Group.

Rick Joyner, *Overcoming Witchcraft*

Rick Joyner of Morning Star Ministries is a spokesman for charismatic restorationist Christianity and one of the more well-known prophet leaders in America.

The attacks of witchcraft come in a series of stings. The successive stings are meant to hit the very place where we have been weakened by the previous stings. In this way they build upon each other until the composite result overwhelms the target. The stings of witchcraft usually come in the following order:

1. Discouragement
2. Confusion
3. Depression
4. Loss of Vision
5. Disorientation
6. Withdrawal

7. Despair

8. Defeat

This process can happen quickly, as it did with Elijah, but it usually works more slowly, which makes it even more difficult to discern. However, if we know the enemy's schemes we will not continue to be a subject to them. When these symptoms begin to make inroads into our lives, we must resist the enemy until he flees. If we do not resist him we will be the ones fleeing, just like Elijah....

In Revelation 12:11 we see that the saints overcome Satan:

1. By the blood of the Lamb,

2. by the word of tier testimony, and

3. by loving not their lives even unto death.

We overcome by the blood of the Lamb as we take our stand on what He has already accomplished for us by the blood of the cross. The victory has already been won, and there is no way that we can lose, as long as we abide in Him.

The word of our testimony is the Scriptures. Every time the enemy challenged Jesus He responded with Scripture, countering the enemy's temptation with God's truth. The word of God is "the sword of the Spirit" (see Ephesians 6:17). With the sword, we can deflect the blows from his deceptive words, as well as attack him. Of all the pieces of armor we are commanded to use, the sword is the only offensive weapon (see Ephesians 6:10–18).

That they "did not love their lives even unto death" (see Revelation 12:11 NKJV), is the utter commitment to follow Him regardless of the price. We are called to take up our crosses daily; to do all things for the sake of the gospel, to no longer live for ourselves but for Him.

To the degree that we remain in self-centeredness, we will be vulnerable to the enemy's attack....

All of these...are required for every spiritual victory. Anything less will fail to bring a complete victory.

Excerpted from *Overcoming Witchcraft* by Rick Joyner, Morning Star Publications and Ministry, 1996, www.morningstarministries.org.

Chapter 6

ANGELS, DEMONS, AND SPIRITUAL WARFARE IN THE BOOK OF ACTS

T HE BOOK OF Acts reflects the same basic spiritual atmosphere and theology on these matters as we find in the first three Gospels. The apostles carry on the same ministry and work. Since the writer of the Book of Acts is the same author as the Gospel of Luke, this should come as no surprise. Interaction with angels and demons is simply part of the narrative.

At the Ascension of Yeshua

In the first chapter of Acts, we read about the first angelic visitation. As the disciples looked up into the sky as Yeshua ascended, the text states,

> Suddenly two men dressed in white stood beside them. "Men of Galilee," they said, "why do you stand here looking into the sky? This same Jesus, who has been taken from you into heaven, will come back in the same way you have seen him go into heaven."
> —ACTS 1:10–11

Here the angels give a foundational message on the return of Yeshua. They fulfill their role as their name indicates—messengers.

Spiritual warfare in response to persecution

In Acts chapter 4 we find Peter and John were released from detention after appearing before the Sanhedrin. They were warned to not speak or teach in the name of Yeshua. But they explicitly refused. The prayer after persecution, mild in this case, is an example of spiritual warfare prayer.

> "Sovereign Lord," they said, "you made the heaven and the earth and the sea, and everything in them. You spoke by the Holy Spirit through the mouth of your servant, our father David: 'Why did the nations rage, and the peoples plot in vain? The kings of the earth rise up, and the rulers band together against the LORD and against his anointed one.' Indeed Herod and Pontius Pilate met together with the Gentiles and the people of Israel in this city to conspire against your holy servant Jesus, whom you anointed. They did what your power and will had decided beforehand should happen. Now, Lord, consider their threats, and enable your servants to speak your word with great boldness. Stretch out your hand to heal and perform signs and wonders through the name of your holy servant Jesus."
>
> —ACTS 4:24–30

We read that after they prayed, the place where they were meeting was shaken. They were filled anew with the Holy Spirit. The result was that they spoke the Word of God boldly. Prayer in such situations is spiritual warfare. Note that they confessed the Word of God. Persecution for the Gospel is a rebellion against the Lord's Anointed, Yeshua. The warfare prayer begins with the faith affirmation of the sovereignty of God and the lordship of Yeshua. On that basis Peter asked for an impartation of the power and authority to speak the Word boldly, with power and authority. Signs and wonders continued to confirm the preaching in the subsequent chapters of Acts. The powers of darkness were pushed back, and ground was taken for the Kingdom by preaching the Gospel with power in the Spirit and with signs and wonders. In addition, this type of prayer itself was part of the advance.

The power of the Spirit and holiness in spiritual warfare

We read of Ananias and Sapphira in Acts 5:1–11. One of the tactics of the evil one is to invade the believing community through temptation. This tactic was effective when Ananias and Sapphira fell into the sin of coveting and lying about their giving. The presence and power of God can be a danger to one in serious sin and can also reinforce righteousness. So when both, one after the other, fell dead after a prophetic word where their sin was exposed, "Great fear seized the whole church and all who heard these events" (v. 11). This strengthened resistance to sin. I want to note here that the gift of prophecy exercised through Peter and the immediate judgment from God was also part of spiritual warfare.

Angelic visitation to release the apostles from jail

In Acts 5:17–42 the apostles were arrested due to the jealousy of the Sadducees. We are not told how many. During the night an angel of the Lord, "opened the prison doors and brought them out" (v. 19, NKJV). He then gave them instructions to stand in the temple courts and to proclaim the message of life to the people. At daybreak they proclaimed the word.

The angel is not only a messenger but can also intervene and deliver by direct supernatural action. There are many stories in missions today and in nations where there is much oppression that are amazingly analogous.

When the Sanhedrin met that morning to bring the apostles before them, they were surprised to find them missing. The jail was securely locked. How can an angel effect such an escape? It is amazing. Then someone came and reported that the apostles were teaching in the temple court.

They were again arrested and again under questioning asserted that they had to obey God and would not refrain from proclaiming the good news. Many wanted to put them to death, but the wise counsel of Gamaliel prevented it. The Sanhedrin had them flogged instead. Note that no angel prevented their flogging! Angelic deliverance and spiritual warfare do not always prevent painful suffering for the sake of the Gospel. Yet the apostles rejoiced to be counted worthy to suffer. The progress of the Kingdom continued as they never stopped their work of proclamation and teaching.

Simon the sorcerer in Samaria

Chapter 8 presents the account of Simon the sorcerer. Samaria would have been an area were greater compromise was possible due to some of the pagan influences in Samaritan history. We read that Simon amazed the people and boasted that he was someone great. The people called him "The divine power known as the Great Power" (v. 10, BSB). Even so, the preaching of Philip the deacon was successful and many were baptized including Simon. However, they were not immersed in the Spirit until Peter and John came. They laid hands on them and the Spirit was given. Simon then offered to pay money so that he could duplicate what he saw Peter and John do. This shows how much pagan ideas still influenced him. Peter strongly rebuked him, and Simon then asked Peter to pray for him. It is interesting that Peter did not cast out demonic spirits in dealing with Simon but repentance seemed to be accepted as adequate. I can say from my own experience, that bringing the person to real repentance is the key to deliverance after which the demonic spirits can be commanded to leave with much greater ease.

After this these events, Phillip is told by an angel of the Lord to go to the desert road that goes from Jerusalem to Gaza. This was quite a trip. On his way he met the Ethiopian eunuch who was an important official in the government of the queen of Ethiopia. The Bible never explains why angels are used as messengers in this way instead of a prophetic word from the Spirit. It is an effective means of communication and impresses the one who receives such a visitation to really follow through. Of course, this is not uncommon in the lands of supernaturalist Christianity but rarer in the West (though not unreported).

The vision of Cornelius

In Acts 10 a righteous Gentile who is connected to the synagogue, Cornelius the Roman centurion, has a vision of an angel. We are told,

> He distinctly saw an angel of God, who come to him and said, "Cornelius! ... Your prayers and gifts to the poor have come up as a memorial offering before God. Now send men to Joppa to bring back a man named Simon who is called Peter. He is staying with Simon the tanner whose house is by the sea."
>
> —Acts 10:3–6

Here the angel brings a message but also very detailed and specific directions. Cornelius obeys the message and sends for Peter, who is specially prepared though a succession of visions to respond to the vision given to Cornelius and to return with the men from Cornelius. When Peter comes Cornelius gives him additional information about the vision, and says, "Suddenly a man in shining clothes stood before me" (v. 30).

The recognition of the authenticity of the angelic visitation prompts Peter to conclude that God does not show favoritism but accepts men from every nation who fear Him and do what is right. The supernatural quality of the angelic visitation and the outpouring of the Spirit with signs following in Acts 10:46 convinces Peter that the Gentiles who embrace God are accepted and can be part of the believing community.

Peter's miraculous escape from jail

Acts 12:1–19 parallels Acts 5:19–20. This is another supernatural account. King Herod had already put Jacob (James), the brother of John, to death. During the Feast of Unleavened Bread (Passover) he arrested Peter and had him guarded by four squads of four soldiers. Herod intended a public trial after the Passover. We read that that Church was earnestly praying to God for him. The night before his trial, when sleeping between two soldiers, bound with two chains, and sentries standing guard at the entrance, an angel of the Lord appeared to Peter and a light shone in the cell. He woke Peter up. The chains fell off Peter's wrists.

The angel told Peter to dress, wrap his cloak around him, and to follow him. Peter did so. For Peter, it was unclear whether all that was happening was real. He thought maybe it was only a vision. When they passed the first and second guards, they came to the iron gate at the entrance to the prison and it opened for them. After walking the length of one street, the angel left him. Peter realized at this point that the whole thing was real and states, "Now I know without a doubt that the Lord has sent his angel and rescued me from Herod's clutches and from everything the Jewish people were hoping would happen" (v. 11).

When Peter returned to the house of Mary the mother of John Mark and knocked on the door, the servant girl Rhoda was so overjoyed at the sound of Peter's voice that she neglected to open the door. Some said, "It must be his angel" (v. 15). Does this mean that they thought he had died? Or was it an angel in another sense? But Peter kept on knocking and they let him in. Peter described the whole thing and told them to tell Jacob (James) the brother of Jesus. He then left.

There was great commotion at the jail when the soldiers could not find Peter. Herod had them put to death.

Not only does this account give us information about what an angel can do, but also gives us understanding of what prayer can do. Therefore it is a text on spiritual warfare. For in 12:12 we find that there was a gathering for prayer, no doubt praying on the situation of Peter's imprisonment. **I believe that the implication of the text is that the prayer meeting was effective in bringing deliverance.** However, in spiritual warfare there are casualties. Jacob the brother of John was killed. Perhaps there was no time to pray. We do not know why sometimes there is such a miraculous answer to prayer with deliverance and sometimes martyrdom. The early Church claimed that the blood of the martyrs was itself a type of spiritual warfare. Tertillian said it this way: "The blood of Christians is seed."

Herod comes to his end when he allows himself to receive worship from the pagan representatives from Tyre and Sidon. We read that an angel of the Lord struck him down and he was eaten by worms. Therefore an angel can bring a direct judgment.

Spiritual warfare and authority in Cyprus

The missionary journey of Barnabas, Paul, and John Mark began with supernatural power. In Acts 13:4–12 we read when they came to Paphos they had an audience with Sergius Paulas, the ruler (proconsul) who wanted to hear the word of God. They were opposed by a false prophet-sorcerer, Elymas. He sought to turn the proconsul way from the message. Paul looked at Elymas, and filled with the Spirit and authority said,

> You are a child of the devil and an enemy of every-thing that is right! You are full of all kinds of deceit and trickery. Will you never stop perverting the right ways of the Lord? Now the hand of the Lord is against you. You are going to be blind, and for a time, not even able to see the light of the sun. Immediately a midst and darkness came upon him and he groped about.
>
> —ACTS 13:10–11

When the proconsul saw this, he believed, not only because of the power of God but also the teaching about the Lord.

Spiritual warfare for the progress of the Gospel is here accomplished by a powerful prophetic pronouncement that broke the resistance from a false prophet magician. One of the key types of spiritual warfare reported in world missions is power encounter, where the supernatural forces of Yeshua's emissaries overcome the supernatural forces of pagan and occult power.

The chapters continue with the story of the power of the Gospel with signs and wonders following the preaching. **Warfare against the powers of evil is primarily connected to the preaching of the Gospel with power and wonderful signs and wonders and sometimes with direct confrontation with demonic power as part of this.** However, the demonic power confronted is operating though specific individuals. **We read of no preparation though binding territorial spirits, princes of darkness or fallen archangels.**

Paul and the slave girl with the demonic spirit of false prophecy

The account of Paul and the slave girl in Acts 16:16–24 is instructive. As Paul and his company were going to the place of prayer, they were met by a slave girl who had a spirit through which she predicted the future. She was the source of much income for her owners through her fortune telling. She followed Paul and his company and proclaimed, "These men are servants of the Most High God, who are telling you the way to be saved" (v. 17). She kept this up for many days. One could think that this was beneficial, but Paul knew it was from the wrong spirit. So Paul turned around and said to the spirit, "In the name of Jesus Christ I command you to come out of her!" (v.18). At that moment the spirit left her. We remember that the disciples reported that they could command the demonic spirits to leave people. **Such deliverance confrontations are part of spiritual warfare.**

There was no immediate larger victory from this power encounter. Indeed, the owners were angry about their loss of income. They brought Paul to the marketplace to face the magistrates and accused them of supporting unlawful

141

customs. The crowd agreed and joined in the attack. Paul and Silas were stripped and beaten and were thrown into prison. The prison warden put them in an inner prison and fastened their feet in the stocks. At midnight when Paul was worshipping and singing hymns there was a violent earthquake. The foundations of the prison were shaken and all the prison doors flew open and everyone's chains came off. We are not told that there was angelic involvement, but it is very possible. **Simply worshipping in a time of great trial here could be understood as a powerful means of spiritual warfare.**

The proclamation of the one true God as spiritual warfare

Spiritual warfare in the Hebrew Scriptures is very connected to the battle against idolatry. The issue at that time was for Israel to resist the temptation to become like the nations. In the account of Paul at Athens in Acts 17:16–34, in his address on the Areopagus, he proclaims the foolishness of believing that the God who made the world lived in temples made with hands (the pagan gods do not explain the creation of the world) but that one God created human beings and is the Lord of the heavens and the earth. This part of his speech was somewhat received. Then Paul proclaimed the resurrection of Yeshua. Some ridiculed the idea of the resurrection of the dead. Some also believed. This very proclamation and **the spread of the Gospel as vanquishing paganism is the major foundation of spiritual warfare in Acts and the Epistles.**

The amazing ministry in Ephesus

Paul had special favor in his Ephesian ministry. We do not read of angels and demons and explicit deliverance as primary in the extension of the Kingdom in Ephesus, but the supernatural character of this ministry was quite amazing. Paul's anointed teaching was a key part of spiritual advance. He had three months in the synagogue. For two years after this, he lectured in the lecture hall of Tyrannus. One of the keys to the extension and the triumph of the Gospel were based in those lectures, "God did extraordinary miracles through Paul, so that even handkerchiefs and aprons that had touched him were taken to the sick, and their illnesses were cured and the evil spirits left them" (Acts 19:11–12).

We do read an interesting account about some Jews who sought to have a ministry of driving out evil spirits. They sought to invoke the name of Yeshua over the demonized saying, "In the name of Jesus whom Paul preaches, I command you to come out" (v. 13). This was not a normal pattern of Jewish exorcism. So perhaps they patterned themselves after deliverance ministry as exemplified by Paul and his fellow ministers. When seven sons of Sceva, a Jewish high priest, were doing this, they encountered a more powerful evil spirit who answered them, "Jesus I know, and I know about Paul, but who are you" (v. 15). After this we read that the spirit jumped on them (through the man they were ministering to) and overpowered them all. We read that he gave them a great beating such that the seven ran out of the house naked and bleeding.

This passage has important implications about evil spirits. There are some that are very powerful, and a minister has to walk in real anointing and authority in Yeshua to deal with them. If there is merely a magical approach to using the name of Yeshua, without a real grounded faith relationship, there is great danger. We do know many credible stories of demonic power doing feats of supernatural strength through those who are demonized. This incident actually caused the name of Jesus to be held in higher honor. We read of the following triumph in spiritual warfare.

> Many of those who believed now came and openly confessed what they had done. A number who had practiced sorcery brought their scrolls together and burned them publicly. When they calculated the value of the scrolls, the total came to fifty thousand drachmas. In this way the word of the Lord spread widely and grew in power.
>
> —ACTS 19:18–20

This was a great victory in spiritual warfare. However, there was a great backlash as the silversmiths rose up against Paul and claimed that they were in danger of losing their living. Their way to end the influence of Paul was to claim that the temple of the great goddess Artemus would be discredited. This led to a riot. However, Roman government prevailed and produced order.

SUMMARY OF THE BOOK OF ACTS

The Book of Acts is a very important text for angels, demons, and spiritual warfare. The primary emphasis is on the progress of the Kingdom against the powers of darkness through the preaching of the good news with anointed power and with signs and wonders following. The renouncing of idols and baptism as steps in leaving the realm of darkness and entering the Kingdom of light is important. Though it is not explicitly stated, the cleansing meaning of baptism was certainly understood as releasing people from evil powers. However, there are times in the Book of Acts when direct confrontation with demonic spirits are important in the progress of the Gospel and the extension of the Kingdom of God. United prayer is important in bringing victory in difficult situations, including Peter's incarceration. In addition, worship in jail preceded the earthquake and brought a great victory when Paul and Silas were in jail in Philippi.

We do not find any of the apostles or prophets of the Book of Acts addressing the more powerful princes of darkness over cities, regions, or territories. It seems that prayer and the preaching of the Gospel with anointed power was sufficient to weaken these powers of darkness as noted in Luke 10 when Yeshua saw Satan fall like lightning from heaven. The Bible does not command us to not engage in such activity, but we will have to look further to support this. So far the New Testament has said little about ruling powers over territories. There will be more information on this in the writings of Paul and the Book of Revelation.

Acts provides us with important information on the power of evil spirits when the minister is not really anointed and does not come with the authority of Yeshua. Hence the important story in Acts 19 on the sons of Sceva. In addition, the activity of angels, not only as messengers but also as beings that can supernaturally intervene and aid in producing amazing victories, as Peter's escape from prison, provide us with important information.

EXCURSUS

George Otis Jr., *Informed Intercession*

I personally consider the writings of George Otis Jr. to be the most important on the nature of the demonic realm, the nature of spiritual warfare, and demonology writing in the last fifty years.

This is one of the most important books on spiritual warfare, spiritual mapping, etc. By spiritual mapping, the author is including the whole matter of the roots of demonic covenants; practices in a town, city, or region; idols; shrines; occult leaders; and more. After gaining an understanding of these roots and present practices, fasting and prayer, joint worship, repentance, unity meetings, and praying to God against the powers of darkness that are revealed to be oppressing and blinding, can break the powers. Here are two stories.

> The Umuofai kindred are spread out in several villages situated near the town of Umuahia in Abia State in southeastern Nigeria....
>
> Two Christian brothers, Emeka and Chinedu Nwankpa, had become increasingly distressed over the spiritual condition of their people. While they did not know everything about the Umuofai kindred, or their immediate Ubakala clan, they knew enough to be concerned. Not only were there few Christians but there was also an almost organic connection with ancestral traditions of sorcery, divination and spirit appeasement....
>
> Taking the burden before the Lord, the younger brother, Chinedu Nwankpa, was led into a season of spiritual mapping. After conducting a partial 80-day fast, he learned that his primary assignment...was to spend one day a week with clan elders investigating the roots of prevailing idolatry—including the role of ancestors and shrines. He would seek to understand how and when the Ubakala clan entered into animistic bondage. According to the older brother Emeka, a practicing lawyer and international Bible teacher, this understanding was critical....Emeka responded, "When a people publicly

renounce their ties to false gods and philosophies, they make it exceedingly undesirable for the enemy to remain in their community."

The study was completed in late 1996. ...The brothers soon felt prompted to invite kindred leaders and other interested parties to attend a special meeting.

...The meeting place was not only filled with 300 people, but the audience also included several prominent clan leaders and witch doctors.... Emeka recalls, "[A] young man preaches for exactly 42 minutes. He brings a clear gospel message. He gives a biblical teaching on idolatry and tells the people what it does to a community....He gives a direct altar....Sixty-one adults respond, including people from lines... [of] the traditional priesthood....

There is a local spirit that is supposed to give fertility to the earth. The people of the community believed this particular spirit favoured farmers who planted yams—an old uncle to the potato. A male from each generation was dedicated to this spirit to insure his blessing. When this priest was ready to die, he had to be taken outside so that the heavenly alignment could be undone. He was buried in the night with his head covered with a clay pot. Then, a year after the burial, the skull was exhumed and put in the shrine. These skulls and other sacred objects were never allowed to touch the ground. Of course, sacrifices were also made from time to time....

When the minister finished the altar call, the Nwankpa brothers were startled to see a man coming forward with the sacred skull in his hand. Here in front of them was the symbol of the clan's ancestral power....Eight other spiritual custodians had also come forward.

As Emeka was called forward to pray for these individuals, the Holy Spirit descended on the gathering and all the clan leaders were soundly converted. The new converts were then instructed to divide up into individual family units—most were living near the village of Mgbarrakuma—and enter a time of repentance within the family. This took another hour and twenty minutes. During this time people were in deep conviction, many rolling on the ground, weeping....

After leading this corporate repentance, Emeka heard the Lord say, "It is now time to renounce the covenants made by and for this community over the last 300 years." [After this prayer time] the Lord spoke to [Emeka] again.... He said, "It is now time to go and deal with the different shrines." ...

One of [the] priests, an elder named Odogwu-ogu, stood before the shrine of a particular spirit called Amadi....

"Listen, Amadi, the people who own the land have arrived to tell you that they have just made a new covenant with the God of heaven. Therefore all the previous covenants you have made with our ancient fathers are now void...so it is time for you to return to wherever you came from."

...And then we went through eight more shrines, gathering all the sacred objects and piling them high. [This all was burned with the fetishes in the homes of the people.]...

..."Today," Emeka says, "everybody goes to church." [Good things have begun to happen on all levels]....

[One case study] is Kiambu, Kenya, one-time ministry graveyard, located 14 kilometers northwest of Nairobi. In the late 1980s, after years of profligate alcohol abuse, untamed violence and grinding poverty, the Spirit of the Lord was summoned to Kiambu by a handful of intercessors operating out of a grocery store basement known as the "Kiambu Prayer Cave."

According to Kenyan pastor Thomas Muthee, the real break though came when believers won a high-profile power encounter with a local witch named Mama Jane. Whereas people used to be afraid to go out at night, they now enjoy one of the lowest crime rates in the country. Rape and murder are virtually unheard of. The economy has also started to grow. And new buildings are sprouting up all over town.

...Pastor Muthee [has] seen [his] church grow to 5,000 members—a remarkable development in a city that had never before seen a congregation of more than 90 people....Other community fellowships are growing as well. "There is no doubt," Thomas declares, "that prayer broke the power of witchcraft over this city. Everyone in the community now has a high respect for us. They know that God's power chased Mama Jane from town."

Excerpts are from *Informed Intercession* by George Otis Jr., copyright © 1999. Used by permission of Sentinel Group, http://www.sentinelgroup.org/books.html.

George Otis Jr., *The Last of the Giants*

The following is a clear passage on the nature of the kind of information that leads to greater information for spiritual mapping, that leads to the fasting and prayer to break the spiritual power over territories.

There is no evidence that satanic powers have any natural predilection for particular geographical areas or ethnic groupings. That demonic activity is more pronounced in certain regions and among certain peoples today is due to the fact that spiritual "beech-heads" have been established there by previous generations. At some time in one fashion or another, human beings welcomed evil spirits to dwell among them.

In most of these enemy strongholds, the scope and intensity of demonic control seem to exist in direct proportion to the explicitness of the original welcome, and to the care taken to sustain the spiritual allegiance through various festivals, rites, and pilgrimages.

The fact that mountainous areas manifest a high degree of demonic activity is no arbitrary phenomenon. As Asian studies scholar Edwin Bernbaum observes, "People have traditionally revered mountains [as] places of sacred poer and spiritual atonement." Among [them] are the isolated Qollahuaya people of northeastern Bolivia who treat nearby Mount Kaata very much like a human being. "Rather than pray to it," Bernbaum reveals, "they feed it, stuffing llama fat into holes and caves and pouring sacrificial blood onto earth shrines."

In midsummer months, Japanese artists and "divine-possession clubs" climb Mount Ontake—the Mountain of Trance, in order to be incarnated by Shinto gods. Elsewhere, in remote Tibet, Hindus and Buddhists trek dangerous mountain passes to bathe in the icy waters of Manasarovar, the Lake of the Mind before gazing on holy Mount Kailas, the realm of the highest gods.

The Himalayan Mountain range may represent the world's densest concentration of spiritism. In all the nations skirting these icy behemoths,

Nepal, India, Bhutan, China, Pakistan, and Tibet, overt demonic manifestations are commonplace. According to eyewitness accounts from long-term resident missionaries in Nepal, Christian workers have been bitten (with resultant puncture wounds) and had food supplies eaten by evil spirits. On other occasions, mysterious lights perched atop high mountain peaks have come hurtling down toward their residences only to be driven off by urgent rebukes in the name of Christ.

Excerpts are from *The Last of the Giants* by George Otis Jr., copyright © 1991. Used by permission of Sentinel Group, http://www.sentinelgroup.org/books.html.

Chapter 7

THE PAULINE WRITINGS AND SPIRITUAL WARFARE

THE BOOK OF ROMANS

THE BOOK OF Romans gives limited information on angels and demons. However, it does provide some important information on spiritual warfare. In Paul's theology, Jew and Gentile fell into the bondage of sin. His description of the Gentile world in Romans 1 is a severe evaluation. Into this world of sin, an opportunity has been provided for Jew and Gentile through the death and resurrection of Yeshua plus the gift of the Holy Spirit. Romans 6 is climactic in its description of this deliverance. The believer in Yeshua has been baptized in Yeshua, meaning that he has died with Him and has been resurrected with Him. In this death and resurrection, he has died to sin and has awakened to new life. Most scholars, I believe rightly, see Paul assuming the fullness of the experience of death and resurrection as taking place during immersion in water. Here are some verses on the freedom that is attained:

> For we know that our old self was crucified with him so that the body of sin might be done away with,

that we should no longer be slaves to sin—because anyone who has died has been freed from sin.
—ROMANS 6:6–7

Count yourselves dead to sin, but alive to God in Christ Jesus." (6:11)
—ROMANS 6:11

For sin shall no longer be your master, because you are not under law, but under grace.
—ROMANS 6:14

You have been set free from sin and have become slaves to righteousness.
—ROMANS 6:18

The whole pattern of Pauline thought from Romans 1 to the climax here is that the believer has been freed from the slavery of sin and has entered into a new life where one is no longer in bondage to sin. Death and resurrection in Yeshua is a real experience of deliverance leading to real freedom to obey God. The grace of God in Paul's writings is never the liberty to sin but includes the undeserved power from God by which we are able to live holy and obedient lives. **Therefore preaching the Gospel, and the response to the Gospel through baptism are the keys for spiritual warfare.** If a person is freed from sin, then by implication they must be freed from demonic control. Hence the theology the early Church teaches that baptism cleanses and delivers from demonic spirits.

Romans 7 and 8 show an ancient Middle Eastern method of parallelism and are repeating the truth of Romans 6 in different terms. Romans 7 again describes bondage to sin. However, one is delivered from the law of sin through the power of the Spirit. He is the one that makes the work of our co-crucifixion with Yeshua effective. The emphasis in chapter 8 is not co-death, though it is briefly covered in 8:3–4 where God by sending His Son condemned sin in the flesh and freed us from its power. This means that "the righteous requirement of the law might be fully met in us, who do not live according to the flesh but according to the Spirit" (8:4). We are now the children of God in a new and deeper way, even more than being created in His image. We are heirs with Messiah.

One text deals with the issue of supernatural powers. Paul writes,

> For I am convinced that neither death nor life, neither angels nor demons, neither the present nor the future, nor any powers, neither height nor depth, nor anything else in all creation, will be able to separate us from the love of God that is in Christ Jesus our Lord.
>
> —ROMANS 8:38–39

For Paul, there are angels and demons. However, we are kept safe through the love of God and these powers will not succeed if they oppose us.

It is interesting to note that Paul's most important book has so very little about the topic of demonic power and dealing with it.

THE CORINTHIAN CORRESPONDENCE

There is significant material in 1 Corinthians 8 and 10 on the issue of food sacrificed to idols and idolatry. Yet, the material is difficult to interpret since at one point Paul seems to say that the idol is nothing and it does not affect the food, but at another point that the food sacrificed or dedicated before idols is being sacrificed or dedicated to demons. The paradox is a reflection of the true nature of the situation.

I don't believe that the passages are contradictory. The first issue is that Paul is arguing that dedicating food to an idol or food that was left over after a sacrifice and sold at a market does not affect the essence of the food. Eating it does not mean that a person eats contamination that brings spiritual oppression to demonic beings.

> We know that "An idol is nothing at all in the world" and "There is no God but one." For even if there are so-called gods, whether in heaven or on earth (as indeed there are many "gods" and many "lords"), yet for us there is but one God, the Father, from whom all things came and for whom we live; and there is but one Lord, Jesus Christ, through whom all things came and through whom we live.
>
> —1 CORINTHIANS 8:4–6

The idol in itself is nothing, though Paul does admit that there are other gods. He will later give his view of the nature of these gods. The issue is not the food but the conscience of one who might be disturbed by eating who does not have mature knowledge and conviction.

> Not everyone possesses this knowledge. Some people are still so accustomed to idols that when they eat such food…their conscience is weak, it is defiled. But food does not bring us near to God, we are no worse off if we do not eat, and no better if we do…. Be careful, however, that the exercise of your rights does not become a stumbling block to the weak.
>
> —1 CORINTHIANS 8:7-9

This becomes more serious if one eats in an idol's temple that was part of the civic fellowship and honor. Unity and loyalty in the city was demonstrated by participation in feast to the city god (gods). A brother could follow another who did this and be so hurt in conscience later that it would be very destructive. This is a sin against the brother. Therefore the rule is to not partake if it will hurt a fellow believer in this way.

In chapter 10 there is a hiatus where Paul speaks of his apostleship and also of the Lord's Supper and of the cup of thanksgiving as a participation in the blood of Yeshua. This is the altar of Yeshua. However, when a sacrifice is offered to an idol, not "that an idol is anything" (10:19), there can be a participation in the altar of the false god. Paul then becomes clear noting that the sacrifices of pagans are offered to demons and that he does not want believers to be participants with demons. Furthermore we cannot drink the cup of the Lord and the cup of demons or have part in both the Lord's table and the table of demons (the pagan temple feast). The rule here is to avoid anything which either is or looks like a participation in paganism.

However, Paul still maintains that the meat is not changed in essence. He finally gives a very clear rule.

> If an unbeliever invites you to a meal and you want to go, eat whatever is put before you without raising questions of conscience. But if anyone says to you, "This has been offered in sacrifice," then do not eat it, both for the sake of the man who told you and for the sake of conscience…the other person's conscience, not yours.
>
> —1 CORINTHIANS 10:27–29

The person who eats should not be denounced if he follows this rule and eats what is set before him without asking questions. This seems to be the meaning of verses 30b and 31. Again, "Whether you eat or drink or whatever you do, do it all for the glory of God. Do not cause anyone to stumble, whether Jews, Greeks or the church of God" (vv. 31–32)

Some have taught that Paul discounts the reality of demons. But I believe this is a wrong interpretation and would also contradict other Pauline texts. The issue is that the essence of the food is not changed by the offering but the context of idolatry is an important consideration. Behind idol worship is the worship of demons.

In 1 Corinthians 11 we read what some scholars consider one of the most difficult to interpret and apply texts. Paul writes, "For this reason the woman ought to have a symbol of authority on her head, because of the angels" (v. 10, NKJV).

Paul will add that a woman's long hair is a sign or covering and is her glory. Therefore it should be covered when she publicly prays or prophesies. Some actually think Paul is quoting opponents and that none of this is his teaching. Yet, this is speculative. There is a possibility that Paul is speaking about the fallen angels and the Jewish tradition that it was fallen angels that had illicit relationships with women in Genesis 6. Hence supernatural beings are tempted by the beauty of women's hair.

This text does not add much to our content other than to say that there is an interaction between supernatural beings—angels and fallen angels—with human beings and our behavior should take this into account.

In 2 Corinthians 4:4 we read, "The god of this age has blinded the minds of unbelievers, so that they cannot see the light of the gospel that displays the glory of Christ, who is the image of God."

The god of this world is in other texts noted as Satan or the devil, who has influence upon those who are in rebelling to God, reinforcing that rebellion. Like Yeshua, Paul believes in a mighty malevolent being (under God's ultimate control), who has authority over demonic hosts and with those hosts blinds the minds of unbelievers. It therefore requires a supernatural work of the Spirit to break through. This comes through prayer and the anointed sharing of the Gospel with signs following.

The reality of the realm of false gods is such that in 2 Corinthians, chapter 6, Paul commands believers to not be unequally yoked together with unbelievers. This would join righteousness and wickedness together. Paul is writing at a time where in the Greek speaking world those who were not Jews or followers of Jesus were committed to pagan worship. This for Paul would be tantamount to seeking to produce harmony between "Christ and Belial" (v. 15). He therefore states, "What agreement is there between the temple of God and idols? For we are the temple of the living God" (v. 16). This is usually applied to marriage but can be any partnership where the believer is compromised in a significant way. One aspect of spiritual warfare is, therefore, to remain pure by not entering into wrong compromising relationships with pagans.

The weapons of our warfare are not carnal

In 2 Corinthians 10:4–5 is one of the most quoted texts on the issue of spiritual warfare. It is important to quote this text in full plus verse 6 which is not as frequently quoted.

> For though we live in the world, we do not wage war as the world does. The weapons we fight with

are not weapons of the world. On the contrary, they have divine power to demolish strongholds. We demolish arguments and every pretension that sets itself up against the knowledge of God, and we take captive every thought to make it obedient to Christ. And we will be ready to punish every act of disobedience, once your obedience is complete.

—2 CORINTHIANS 10:3–6

We dearly wish that Paul had laid out more what he does specifically in waging war. These verses are used by some practitioners of spiritual warfare to argue for prayer and fasting as the weapon to demolish strongholds, which are looked at sometimes as demonic powers over a territory. The text is also used to indicate support for addressing dark powers and commanding them to loose their hold over a territory or over a people group. By addressing them, we demolish their strongholds. Others think that this is reading into the text and that there is nothing in the text that speaks about these kinds of activities. John Wimber, the founder of the Vineyard movement, was known for arguing against addressing the powers of darkness.

The idea of a stronghold is a place of resistance to an enemy army. It is a stone tower or a building. Paul's idea is that the foundationally wrong ideas, commitments, and values are deeply ingrained in human beings. These are strongholds of the mind in individuals and in their culture that resist the truth. They are reinforced by the powers of darkness. **The way these strongholds are demolished is by the anointed preaching of the Gospel with signs following. There is great power in this.** In addition, the presentation of the Word with power also replaces the wrong foundations with the right foundations.

When Paul speaks about arguments, he is speaking about **an anointed apologetic that demolishes false arguments**. Wimber would certainly have accepted that prayer and fasting are weapons to overcome demonic power and to extend the Kingdom of God. I think we need to see that these are weapons of warfare. Wimber, however, strongly rejected addressing higher dark powers and commanding the demons in specific individuals to leave or be bound. Paul does not in this text ask us to ask God to bind the powers of darkness either.

Paul also says that he will punish disobedience. How he can do this is not stated. Will he move to dis-fellowship people? What if he does not have the support of the local congregation? Will there be immediate judgments as with Ananias and Sapphira? We are not told. Earlier in the book, Paul says he will come with power in such a way that it will show up the false teachers and apostles. Supernatural power in some way is implied and indeed could be part of the weapons of warfare. (See 1 Corinthians 2:4; 4:20–21.) In 2 Corinthians 13 Paul does speak about two or three witnesses, so he does have in mind some kind of judicial process? He says he will not spare those who sinned earlier since they are demanding proof that God is speaking through Paul. He states that God is not weak in dealing with them but is powerful among them.

I believe that though Paul does not explicitly mention prayer and fasting here, or worship for that matter, they are weapons of warfare and do release power from God as we have seen from other texts. While I will later speak to the issue of addressing the dark powers over territories, suffice it to say that **nothing I am saying here precludes being led by the Spirit to do things that are not explicitly taught in the Bible. However, this book is about**

what the Bible says. People often think that the practices of their stream of congregations are clearly in the Bible. Sometimes they read into biblical texts.

Paul's thorn in the flesh

Paul was granted amazing experiences in the Spirit, including being caught up to the third heaven where he saw wonderful things. He said that to keep him from becoming conceited he "was given a thorn in my flesh, a messenger of Satan, to torment me" (12:7). He pleaded with the Lord three times to take it away, but the only answer he received was that God's grace was sufficient. Therefore Paul says that he boasts gladly about his weaknesses.

This trial is variously interpreted as different sicknesses (an eye disease, malaria, and epilepsy are the three candidates) or simply the Satanic opposition that always followed Paul to something that is not possible to know. Those who believe that physical healing is an absolute promise do not accept that it was a physical sickness. Whatever it was, the thorn was ultimately from God, though it is called a messenger of Satan. Satan means accuser or one who opposes, and Satan did oppose Paul time after time when the Gospel was spreading through his efforts. The point is that the text points to Satan or his messengers as real, but ultimately controlled by God.

THE BOOK OF GALATIANS

In this important letter Paul argues that Gentiles, those from the nations, are not required to keep the whole Torah (Law). They connect to God through the New Covenant, or the fulfillment of the seed promise in the Messiah. One of the aspects of the superiority of the New Covenant or the fulfilled promise is that it was established by the seed

Himself, so that what was promised is given to those who believe. (See chapter 4:22.) The Law or the Torah on the other hand, "was put into effect through angels by means of a mediator" (Gal. 3:19, HCSB). Paul then says that a mediator does not represent just one party, but God is one. What Paul means here, to my best judgment is that Yeshua as divinity is directly the one who establishes the law of the New Covenant without any mediator. (See Matthew chapters 5 through 7 where Jesus says, "It has been said" and later adds, "but I say to you.") For our purposes, it is interesting that Paul agrees with the tradition that the angels were involved in conveying the details of the Torah to Moses (not the Ten Commandments, which were inscribed by God Himself). Yes, the Torah is the Word of God, but one recognizes the superiority of the New Covenant Torah as it was directly given by the God-Man, Yeshua. It is again important to see that angels function in giving revelation.

In Paul's argument against those who taught that one must keep the whole Law of Moses to be saved, especially here applied to Gentiles (those from the nations), he states,

> Formerly, when you did not know God, you were slaves to those who by nature are not gods. But now that you know God—or rather are known by God—how is it that you are turning back to those weak and miserable forces? Do you wish to be enslaved by them all over again? You are observing special days and months and seasons and years! I fear for you, that somehow I have wasted my efforts on you.
> —GALATIANS 4:8–11

The text becomes more interesting due to some translations that state that they were turning back to "elementary spirits" against the NIV's "weak and miserable principles." It is clear that Paul is saying that these former pagans were in bondage to false gods (or demonic spirits). Yet how could observing days, months, seasons, and years bring them into bondage, especially if these were times of celebration that God gave? This has prompted a number of scholars to hold that these former pagans were taking Jewish calendar times and combining them with a superstitious approach from paganism and perhaps including pagan observances of times and seasons. The verse seems to have language like Deuteronomy that commanded against observance of seasons (meaning pagan superstition on when it was safe to do some things and at other times unsafe). This was the view of the famous charismatic teacher Dr. Derek Prince.

A wrong kind of idolatrous approach to anything can bring us into bondage.

THE BOOK OF EPHESIANS

The closing chapter of Ephesians contains one of the very most important passages on spiritual warfare in the Bible (verses 10 through 20) and also gives us information on the powers of darkness.

Paul first of all says that we are in a struggle, "not against flesh and blood, but, against the rulers, against the authorities, against the powers of this dark world and against the spiritual forces of evil in the heavenly realms" (Eph. 6:12). In addition Paul notes previously that we have to stand against "the devil's schemes" (v. 11).

This is very explicit language. First there is a devil; and whether it is him directly or not, since the word *devil* stands for demonic spirits that may be involved and scheming, is not important. They are plotting temptations that are subtle and into which the believer may succumb.

In addition, they can give wrong direction and inspiration. This is not in the text but is pretty much the meaning of scheming. Paul's view, as many writers in the first century, believed that there is a realm of evil that exercises authority in the lives and locations where people are in rebellion against God. The words "rulers," "powers of this dark world," and "spiritual forces of evil in the heavenly realms" are descriptive terms for evil beings. Rulers imply that some have authority exercised over those given to evil or pagan practices. Powers and spiritual forces may be at various levels in hierarchy, and the words are not determined with regard to status. For a first century Jew like Paul, powers or spiritual forces are all around.

So how does Paul counsel that we resist or overcome these powers of evil? His answer is the full armor of God. When we have this armor on, we can stand! First of all we wear a belt of truth. This means that we are unwavering in standing for the truth revealed in the Bible. In Paul's time the Hebrew Scriptures and the oral tradition about Yeshua and the apostolic teaching of Paul himself were the foundation of truth. The breastplate of righteousness is uncompromising practice of the ways of God in the commandments of Jesus. Our feet are to be fit with the readiness of the Gospel of peace. The meaning is that we have greater protection from falling when we are overtly sharing the Gospel and spreading it to others. Then Paul mentions the shield of faith/faithfulness where we stand on the basis of the promises of God and walk faithfully. The shield of faith is said to extinguish the flaming arrows of the evil one. The exercise of faith would then be to stand on the basis of Scripture. The flaming arrows are accusations, threats, attacks, inspirations to temptation, and more. The shield of faith standing on the Word extinguishes the flaming arrows. This would be parallel to Yeshua quoting the Scripture when the devil sought to tempt Him. The helmet of salvation is the protection of the head on the basis of God's accomplished provision on which we have confidence and a clear conscience. The sword of the Spirit is the Word of God by which we advance the Kingdom and take territory from the realm of evil. This is the proclamation of the Word of God.

Paul adds prayer and all kinds of requests as powerful weapons of warfare. He councils praying in the Spirit, which is probably praying with the gift of tongues. This would relate to Ephesians 5:18 where we are counseled to "be filled with the Spirit" and verse 19 where he tells us to sing spiritual songs. Walking in the fullness of the Spirit is a key to our own spiritual protection and advance.

We note again that this wrestling is not connected to individuals or groups meeting to speak commandments to the powers of darkness.

THE BOOK OF PHILIPPIANS

The Book of Philippians, like much of the Pauline writings, does not speak directly about the battle with demonic powers. However, the teaching on living godly lives in the Messiah is a key to personal and corporate spiritual warfare. This includes our living in humility after the pattern of the Messiah who "emptied himself, by taking the form of a servant. And being found in human form, he humbled himself by becoming obedient" (Phil. 2:7–8, ESV). It includes living in thankfulness or rejoicing in the Lord always and by prayer and petition with thanksgiving making our request to God. This will lead to the peace of God that passes all understanding, guarding our hearts and minds. (See chapter 4, verses 4–6.)

This guarding of our hearts by these means is a key to freedom from dark forces.

THE BOOK OF COLOSSIANS

Salvation is deliverance from darkness. "For he has rescued us from the dominion of darkness and brought us into the kingdom of the Son he loves, in whom we have redemption, the forgiveness of sin" (Col. 1:13–14).

The meaning of this is extended in Colossians 2:13–15. Deliverance from our sins, and the cancelation of the record of our offenses (the regulations that stood against us) has been provided. "And having disarmed the powers and authorities, he made a public spectacle of them, triumphing over them by the cross" (v. 15).

The sense of these verses is that what looked like the ultimate triumph of evil was actually the place of and reality of the defeat of evil. Such power was released by the crucifixion of Yeshua, that He made a public example of these powers. Love triumphed. He triumphed over them by the power released by the Cross. When we embrace and apply the meaning of His crucifixion, we experience that power of overcoming the powers of darkness. Standing on the foundation of His crucifixion brings us freedom.

We are also informed in verse 18 that there was false teaching that humility entailed the worship of angels. There were false visions that supported this false teaching. Angels serve God and His people and are not to be worshipped.

In Colossians 2:20 we read that the Colossians "died with Christ to the elemental spiritual forces of this world." This is interpreted in some translations as spirits. Hence Paul asks,

Why, as though you still belonged to the world, do
you submit to rules: Do not handle! Do not taste! Do
not touch! These rules, which have to do with things
that are all destined to perish with use, are based
on merely human commands and teachings. Such
regulations indeed have an appearance of wisdom,
with their self-imposed worship, their false humility
and their harsh treatment of the body, but they lack
any value in restraining sensual indulgence.

—Colossians 2:20–23

The context has led to some significant controversy since
the paragraph does not describe biblical Torah, which
Paul would not call mere human commands. Therefore
some see this as the legal extensions of Judaism; others
see these as connected to paganism, including the worship of angels above which was not taught by Judaism. The
point here is that liberty and freedom from dark powers
is through identification with the crucifixion of Yeshua.
Paul's language is reminiscent of Romans 6 where liberty
comes from our co-death and resurrection with Yeshua.

On more thought I think is a possible implication of the
idea of Yeshua's death on the cross making a disarmed and
made public example of the powers and authorities. This
would relate to participation in the Lord's Supper. In that
supper we are told by Paul that we show "the Lord's death
until he comes" (1 Cor. 11:26). To whom are we showing
the Lord's death? **If we put the verses in Colossians
together with the verses in 1 Corinthians, it is possible
that every time we take the Lord's supper in unity we
reinforce the disarming of the dark powers. We represent the death of Yeshua and our co-death and release
great supernatural power.** When we partake in unity as a
corporate community we release power. When we partake

as representatives of the unity of the Church of the city, there is power released for the sake of the city. It might be that the Lord's Supper itself, connected to the unity of God's people, is one of the greatest weapons of spiritual warfare. This seems to be the sense of the more ancient churches.

In chapter 3 Paul, as in other Epistles, gives instructions for holy or godly living, for holy living is a key to maintain freedom from the forces of evil. Again, we are to control our minds and to set them on things above.

1 AND 2 THESSALONIANS

Paul does give some limited information on spiritual warfare in the Thessalonian correspondence. In 1 Thessalonians 5 he notes that the Yeshua believers are not in darkness that the day of the Lord (His coming in judgment and salvation) should overtake us as a thief. We are not of the night or darkness but of the light, so we are told to be alert and self-controlled. This is a way to guard ourselves in times of pressure when the temptations could be great. As in Ephesians, faith is a breastplate of protection, but in this case love is included with faith as part of that breastplate of protecting. The hope of salvation again is a helmet. We should not have fear for God has not appointed us for wrath but salvation. So the helmet of salvation is our confidence of salvation in Jesus.

In 2 Thessalonians 2 is an important chapter on the final spiritual warfare between the man of lawlessness who is doomed to destruction and the people of the Kingdom of God. He leads the people of the kingdom of darkness. He will oppose God and worship and will set himself up in God's temple proclaiming himself as God. This is parallel to the worship of Caesar. Is Paul speaking of the literal temple in Jerusalem or a temple of god such as would be known as the center of Roman worship?

This battle between good and evil includes a secret power of lawlessness that is already at work. In one of the most debated texts (verse 7), we are to know what is holding him back or restraining him. There is one interpretation that teaches that we should translate the verse such that the devil is holding back or restraining or opposing the Gospel and will continue to do so until he is taken out of the way in judgment. Whatever the interpretation, we should know that the nature of this last confrontation is spiritual warfare at its height. The final victory will only come with the direct intervention of the Lord who will overthrow him with the breath of His mouth and by the splendor of His coming (v. 8).

The lawless one will be empowered by Satan, with all kinds of counterfeit miracles, signs, and wonders. Signs and wonders will confirm an evil path for those who are deceived and perishing. Because of their evil, God will send them a powerful delusion so they will believe a lie. Those who do not believe the truth and delight in wickedness can thereby be judged.

We should note that these passages fit the picture of last days battles that combine real wars on earth in connection to wars in the heavens as noted in the Book of Revelation. These wars are connected to battles over Israel and God's ancient people, the Jewish people.

The believer's response to all this must be to stand firm and hold to the teachings that came from Paul whether by letter or by word of mouth. In chapter 3 prayer is enjoined as a mighty weapon. Paul specifically asks for prayer to be delivered from evil and wicked men.

1 AND 2 TIMOTHY

Chapter 1 of 1 Timothy begins by speaking to the battle of maintaining sound teaching. This is an essential and requires some to be commanded to not continue to teach false doctrines.

One part of spiritual warfare is summarized in 1 Timothy 2:1–4.

> I urge, then, first of all, that petitions, prayers, intercession and thanksgiving be made for all people— for kings and all those in authority, that we may live peaceful and quiet lives in all godliness and holiness. This is good, and pleases God our Savior, who wants all men to be saved and to come to a knowledge of the truth.

While sometimes persecution and situations of injustice are used by God to extend the Kingdom of God, praying for authorities is very important so that we might have circumstances where the governmental authorities are not trying to thwart the progress of the Gospel. Spiritual warfare can thus be understood by the fact that our prayers do influence those in authority and can turn their hearts toward greater justice.

In chapter 6 we find that the temptation to greed can be a great deception by which one may shipwreck their faith. Keeping ourselves free of deception through subtle false teaching is crucial to the progress of the Kingdom.

> People of corrupt mind, who have been robbed of the truth and who think that godliness is a means to financial gain. But godliness with contentment is great gain....Those who want to get rich fall into temptation and a trap and into many foolish and

harmful desires that plunge people into ruin and destruction. For the love of money is a root of all kinds of evil. Some people, eager for money, have wandered from the faith and pierced themselves with many griefs.

—1 TIMOTHY 6:5–6, 9–10

Timothy is told to "Flee from all this....Fight the good fight of the faith" (vv. 11–12).

In 2 Timothy are told that we are to "endure hardship as a good soldier of Jesus Christ" (2 Tim. 2:3, NKJV). Paul describes this life here as a spiritual battle and also as parallel to an athletic competition. Several exhortations fit the nature of this spiritual warfare. Again, Timothy is told, "Flee the evil desires of youth and pursue righteousness" (v. 22).

We are told, "Everyone who wants to live a godly life in Christ Jesus will be persecuted, while evildoers and impostors will go from bad to worse, deceiving and being deceived" (3:12–13).

So much of this advice is practical advice emphasizing prayer, pursuing righteousness, and avoiding deception by maintaining a firm stand on the foundations of biblical truth.

TITUS

Titus as well provides us with similar teaching on keeping away from deceptive teaching, and divisions and saying no to all ungodly worldly passions and to live godly lives while waiting for the blessed hope, the appearing of Jesus in the His second coming. (See Titus 2:12–14.)

Excursus

George Otis, *The Twilight Labyrinth*
This amazing book on why spiritual darkness lingers where it does is a remarkable manual of the kinds of rituals, evil covenants, idolatries, and traditions that reaffirm pacts with evil. Here are two excepts on spiritual warfare and demonic power.

> The days surrounding religious festivals, pilgrimages and ceremonials are often charged with spiritual intensity. A primary reason for this...is that powerful demonic entities are near and attentive. At the same time, however, these seasons are fragile. From the enemy's perspective, there is always a risk, however small, that people will use these occasions to deny him continued access to the community.
>
> As concerned and knowledgeable intercessors, we want to exploit this very possibility. By rolling up our prayer sleeves during these important events, we aim to bring about conditions that will cause men and women to reconsider the pacts that have enslaved them. As Clinton Arnold reminds us, "A tradition ceases to be a tradition when people no longer pass it on."
>
> To assist intercessors in this task, my own ministry; The Sentinel Group, distributes monthly spiritual counterwarfare calendars that provide details sixty days in advance of spiritually significant events. Offering an illustration of how this kind of prayer can deplete the enemy's fishing hole, Guatemalan teacher-evangelist Francisco Galli recently reported a breakdown of idolatrous pilgrimages in and

around Guatemala City. This occurred when a group of concerned women with United for Prayer, and an intercessory prayer consortium, posted themselves along pilgrimage routes fifteen days before the city's Holy Week processions in 1995.

According to Galli, when one of the more famous (and syncretistic) processions was pulling out of its staging area at Calvary Church, many of the of the people carrying the images fell down and actually broke their arms and legs. Then, when the woman in charge of the procession bent over to retrieve a fallen idol, she immediately suffered a heart attack. Equally dramatic developments were unfolding at the same time at the other staging areas. In one episode, reminiscent of the scene recorded in the Philistine temple of Dagon, an idol toppled over of its own accord and was decapitated. At another location, the central idol spontaneously caught fire. In a neighboring town, the processional images were left in their crypts because the celebrants were afraid to carry them.

As a consequence of three events, a number of Guatemalans have begun to question their long association with traditional gods. New evangelical congregations have been springing up from the capital to the highlands—a distressing development for demonic powers that have trolled these fishing grounds for millennia....

Roberto Iztep (is) a practicing shaman and leader in the Mayan revitalization movement....

While we ate, three men gave brief talks on the importance of serving Waxaqib Batz' and honoring the day gods. When they finished, a male dancer emerged from the shadows in a masked jaguar costume. Pantomiming the cat's movements, he rose occasionally to strike a drum tucked precariously under one arm. After ten minutes he beckoned me. When I smiled benignly, he moved closer with mock menace. As the other guests giggled nervously, the performer began to "bite" into my arm. Overwhelmed by the small of alcohol on his breath, I was suddenly unsure where this would lead.

A few minutes later we discovered that we were being tested. The shaman had been watching us for some time. We also learned that the main New Year's activities did not start until six A.M., although a smaller preparatory ceremony would be held around midnight. We were welcome to observe....

The sacred summit at his center (is) called Paklom, this modest hill hosts the most revered site in the Momostekan world—a place known as the Waquibal, or "Six-Place." Those who worship here do so in the belief that they are standing at the very axis of the universe...

The worshipers...formed a semicircle around a concrete hearth crowned by three sooty crosses. As the shaman paused to collect and offering for his services...a young mother seized the occasion to lay her swaddled infant in a makeshift bed of straw. It was a fateful decision.

At eleven P.M. the ceremony began in earnest. Lighting a fire in the hearth, Iztep launched into a lengthy prayer designed to close out unfinished business with all 260 Mayan day deities. Despite the repetitive nature of the entreaty, the crowd stayed glued to the process. Like most Maya traditionalists, they were convinced that to carry broken vows into the new year is to invite serious economic or physical distress.

Iztep's actions, however, were not merely confessional. As an authentic shaman, he was also endeavoring to create a portal that would rejoin the human world to the Otherworld. He called this sacred, universal space..."the glory hole." ...It was here that he had to receive and pass on a blessed substance known as *itz* (derived from the god *Itzamna*). According to archaeologist David Freidel, *itz* represents the flowing liquid of heaven and is manifest in such things as morning dew, human tears, the sap of a tree...and melting candle wax....

With midnight nearly upon us, the ceremony was reaching a climax. Pivoting to the cardinal directions, Iztep and the worshipers, some of whom were fully entranced, called forth spiritual legions to receive their oblation. As Paklom was transformed into a spiritual vortex, the arrival of unseen spirits became palpable.

Suddenly, as if on cue, a pack of wild, snarling dogs appeared on the opposite side of the hill. I knew instantly why they had come. Still, watching them make a beeline for the sleeping infant sparked deep indignation. Striding toward the vicious dogs, several of whom were already tugging at the little bundle in the hay, I rebuked the controlling spirits.

The effect was dramatic. In a split second the deadly spell was shattered and the snarling pack was transformed into a benign gaggle of wagging tails. Interrupted by divine power, the perverse passion play came to an abrupt halt. The child's mother, oblivious to the peril that had brushed up against her, shook off her trance and disappeared with her baby into the night.

Excerpts are from *The Twilight Labyrinth* by George Otis, copyright © 1997. Used by permission of Sentinel Group, http://www.sentinelgroup.org/books.html.

Chapter 8

HEBREWS AND THE GENERAL EPISTLES AND SPIRITUAL WARFARE

THE BOOK OF HEBREWS AND ANGELS

THERE IS NO unity on who authored the Book of Hebrews. Some of the teaching seems closer to John and some to Paul. Some see Barnabus or Apollos as the author and others an unknown author.

Hebrews gives a significant role to angels. In the very first chapter the writer says,

> When God brings his firstborn into the world, he says, "Let all God's angels worship him." In speaking of angels he says, "He makes his angels spirits, and his servants flames of fire." But about the Son he says, "Your throne, O God, will last forever and ever."
>
> —HEBREWS 1:6–7

The comparison is to the Son, Jesus, who is far superior to the angels. Hebrews is very strong in teaching the deity of Jesus. (See Hebrews 1:1–3.) In verse 4 we read after His ascension, "he became as much superior to the angels as the name he has inherited is superior to theirs."

And in verses 13 and 14 we read,

> To which of the angels did God ever say, "Sit at
> my right hand until I make your enemies a foot-
> stool for your feet"? Are not all the angels minis-
> tering spirits sent to serve those who will inherit
> salvation?

Immediately we know from this that angels serve God, that Yeshua the Messiah is more exalted, and that the angels are to minister or serve in various ways those who will inherit salvation. This can be, as we saw earlier in the Book of Acts, for protection and for revelation.

In chapter 2 we read that we must pay careful attention to God's teaching through Yeshua and His representatives,

> For since the message spoken by angels was binding,
> and every violation and disobedience received its
> just punishment, how shall we escape if we ignore
> such a great salvation?
>
> —HEBREWS 2:2–3

The idea here is that the angels were involved in con-veying the content of Torah to Moses.

Indeed, God put everything under Yeshua's feet, not angels. (See verses 5–8.)

In Hebrews 2:14 we read that Yeshua shared in our "humanity so that by his death he might break the power of him who holds the power of death—that is, the devil—and free those who all their lives were held in slavery by their fear of death."

The devil brought death into the world and desires to destroy humanity. Hence he keeps human beings in dark-ness so that they are headed to destruction and not to life.

Hebrews 12:22 reminds us of Ephesians 2 which states that we have been raised with Him and are seated with

Him in heavenly places. In a spiritually connected way we are there.

> You have come to Mount Zion, to the city of the living God, the heavenly Jerusalem. You have come to thousands upon thousands of angels in joyful assembly, to the church of the firstborn, whose names are written in heaven.

This idea that there are myriads of angels serving God in heaven is an important glimpse into heavenly reality. It makes sense of the very title of God, The LORD of hosts, where hosts can mean armies and is referring most probably to heavenly armies as seen by Elijah and not merely to the armies of Israel.

THE GENERAL EPISTLES

The Book of James (Jacob)

James tells us that there are two types of wisdom—godly wisdom and devilish wisdom. Devilish wisdom provides the intelligence to fulfill envy and selfish ambition. We sometimes are amazed at how insidiously effective evil schemes can be.

> Such "wisdom" does not come down from heaven but is earthly, unspiritual, demonic. For where you have envy and selfish ambition, there you find disorder and every evil practice.
>
> —JAMES 3:15–16

We must resist temptations to envy and selfish ambition and instead pursue the wisdom that comes from heaven which produces behavior that "is first of all pure; then peace-loving, considerate, submissive, full of mercy and good fruit, impartial and sincere" (v. 17).

In addition we are told,

> Submit yourselves, then, to God. Resist the devil, and he will flee from you Come near to God and he will come near to you. Wash your hands, you sinners, and purify your hearts, you double minded....Humble yourselves before the Lord, and he will lift you up.
>
> —JAMES 4:7-8, 10

Prayer, humbling, and repentance are the means of deliverance.

The Epistles of Peter

In 1 Peter 5:8–9 we read,

> Be alert and of sober mind. Your enemy the devil prowls around like a roaring lion looking for someone to devour. Resist him, standing firm in the faith, because you know that the family of believers throughout the world are undergoing the same kind of sufferings.

How is this victory over the devil accomplished? First of all, by being alert. We should know that in persecution—the context here—or in times of relative quiet there are various kinds of temptation, some very subtle, that are inspired by demonic forces, usually through other people but sometimes directly. In persecution we are tempted to give up or renounce our faith or to doubt the goodness of God. In times of quiet we can be complacent and let our guards down. **All of the moral instruction of how we are to live is a part of spiritual warfare.** With regard to persecution, Peter again says to be "strong, firm and stead-fast" (v. 10). The power comes from Him.

In 2 Peter 2, Peter notes that "God did not spare the angels when they sinned, but sent them to hell, putting them into gloomy dungeons to be held for judgment" (2 Pet. 2:4). This passage gives us pause. Where are the fallen angels? Are they somewhere in the air causing temptation? Are they under the earth but somehow able to leave and cause temptation? Are they held in a place? If so, how are they involved in the demonic activity that is also described? Or is it only some fallen angels who are held in a gloomy dungeon waiting for judgment? Or is the gloomy dungeon the characteristic of their lives and not really a specific place? We could wish there was more information. This verse seems to be contrary to other verses. There are ways to reconcile this with the other verses, but to do so is to speculate.

Verses 10 through 12 provide us with instructions on humility. The bold and arrogant men are not afraid to slander celestial beings. Are these fallen angels? For who would be slandering non-fallen angels, celestial beings? We then read that angels who "are greater in power and might, do not bring a reviling accusation against them before the Lord" (v. 11, NKJV).

Some people think that this defines spiritual warfare as precluding addressing supernatural demonic beings with accusations of their evil or even addressing them at all. This is by others only applied to ruling evil spirits. The whole subject of addressing demonic ruling spirits will be addressed at the end of this book. This is a source of controversy. Here we would at least conclude that spiritual warfare should be engaged with humility.

The Epistles of John

In these Epistles the issue is resisting antichrist. In his first Epistle, chapter 2, John tells us that we have an anointing that can warn us when false teaching is coming. We sense a check and that something is wrong. The man who denies that Jesus the Messiah has come in the flesh is the antichrist. He is one that denies both the Father and the Son. If one denies the Son, he does not have the Father.

Most believe that John is dealing with an early type of Gnosticism (proto-Gnosticism) that rejected the value of the physical world and hence denied the incarnation. It appears that John teaches the future coming of one ultimate antichrist figure but that there are several such figures before the ultimate one.

In chapter 4 John gives us a test of spirits.

> Dear friends, do not believe very spirit, but test the spirits to see whether they are from God, because many false prophets have gone out into the world. This is how you can recognize the Spirit of God. Every spirit that acknowledges that Jesus Christ has come in the flesh is from God, but every spirit that does not acknowledge Jesus is not from God. This is the spirit of the antichrist, which you have heard is coming and even now is already in the world. You, dear children, are from God, and have overcome them, because the one who is in you is greater than the one who is in the world....We are from God, and whoever knows God listens to us; but whoever is not from God does not listen to us. This is how we recognized the Spirit of truth and the spirit of falsehood.
>
> —1 JOHN 4:4–5, 6

In these important verses we learn about the ability of the Holy Spirit to help us discern people that come with false teaching that deny the incarnation. Testing the spirits is part of our spiritual warfare.

Antichrists point to a future ultimate figure. False teachers are of the spirit of antichrist. John as well sees demonic spirits behind this false teaching.

John' second Epistle repeats the same teaching on false teaching: "Many deceivers who do not acknowledge Jesus Christ as coming in the flesh, have gone out into the world. Any such person is the deceiver and the antichrist" (2 John 1:7).

In this case the issue is continuing in the teaching that they were originally given.

The letter from Jude (Judah)

The sense of warfare in Jude is focused on maintaining the faith that was delivered.

> I felt compelled to write and urge you to contend for the faith that was once for all entrusted to God's holy people. For certain individuals whose condemnation was written about long ago have secretly slipped in among you. They are ungodly people, who pervert the grace of our God into a license for immorality and deny Jesus Christ our only Sovereign and Lord.
>
> —JUDE 1:3-4

This is one of the later sins of libertarian Gnosticism that taught that we can continue to sin in body because the body is not significant. Furthermore, we can continue to sin, according to this false teaching, because we are saved by grace. Warfare again is connected to contending for the truth.

Jude 1:6 repeats the same teaching as Peter in regard to fallen angels and states in somewhat different terms the following.

> And the angels who did not keep their positions of authority but abandoned their proper dwelling— these he has kept in darkness, bound with everlasting chains for judgment on the great Day.

Some think this would be speaking of those angels who cohabited with women and that the meaning of the sons of God marrying the daughters of men had to do with the giants in the earth leading to the flood. Sexual immorality and perversion are noted in the text. There is strong evidence for an ancient Jewish interpretation for this understanding and, strange as it seems, it is possible. Indeed, he connects the fallen angels in the same text to the kind perversion present in Sodom and Gomorrah.

In verse 8, we read that those who rebel against God's ways, "pollute their own bodies, reject authority and heap abuse on celestial beings." We are not told just how they are slandering these beings. Were angels or fallen angels involved? We ask these questions as well in the Peter passage above.

Michael the archangel is now put forth as an example of humility. We read about Michael in the Book of Daniel. Then we read an account from the apocryphal literature, not inspired Scripture, but which Jude quotes as a worthy example of truth.

> But even the archangel Michael, when he was disputing with the devil about the body of Moses,

did not dare to bring to condemn him for slander but said, "The Lord rebuke you." Yet these people slander whatever they do not understand.

—JUDE 1:9–10

This verse has led some to strongly oppose directly addressing princes of darkness and rebuking them or commanding them to release territories where they have influence. Those who believe in such activity say that human beings in the power of Yeshua have more authority than angels. Yet the point of the passage is to be an example for people.

The text then gives a quote from the book of Enoch which is not Scripture and certainly not an actual writing from Enoch. However, Jude may have believed that this text did enshrine true prophecy. Perhaps Enoch appeared in a vision and gave a prophetic word. We will never be able to solve this mystery. He writes:

> Enoch, the seventh from Adam, prophesied about them: "See, the Lord is coming with thousands upon thousands of his holy ones to judge everyone, and to convict all of them of all the ungodly acts they have committed in their ungodliness, and of all the defiant words ungodly sinners have spoken against him."

—JUDE 1:14–15

This text fits the idea that the Lord is the Lord of hosts, or angelic armies. There is some evidence, however, that the Lord's coming with His saints is intending His return with those who have died and will be resurrected. (See Revelation 19:19; Daniel 12:2)

We are to resist scoffers who follow their own desires and bring false doctrine to divide us. These are said to follow mere natural instincts.

EXCURSUS

Cindy Jacobs, *Deliver Us from Evil*

Cindy Jacobs important book *Deliver us from Evil* provides a compendium of the kinds of involvements that bring oppression and demonization. Spiritual warfare requires deliverance from evil by repenting of and renouncing such involvements, individually and corporately. This can lead to warfare against the powers of darkness in our communities. Beyond the normal methods of corporate prayer warfare noted in many of the books noted in this book, Cindy Jacobs also recommends public action to remove occult influences.

> A very powerful weapon against the occult invasion in our society is letter writing. Television networks are very much influenced by public opinion. If you see an objectionable show on a certain network, write a letter and object to the content. Even one letter can kick up quite a bit of dust. Write to the mayor, school-board members and local newspapers. Remember the influence one woman named Madalyn Murray O'Hair had on our society. She was the driving force behind prayer being taken out of American public schools in 1962.
>
> I believe that God is raising up men and women of God who are not afraid to stand up and protect our society against the occult influences we

see today! We are not out to persecute the Wiccans or any other sin the occult. We love those who are Wiccans and do not want any harm to come to them. However, we also know that what they teach does not please God....

> Christians, the last word for is for us. We must intercede. We must stand our ground against Satan and the occult. But as we do this, we must remember that God loves every Wiccan, every soothsayer, everyone who has ever read a horoscope, everyone who has played Dungeons and Dragons and anyone who has dabbled in any aspect of the occult. Let's pray for them and be ready to extend open arms to them when they do come to seek the truth of the one true God.

Cindy Jacobs, *Deliver Us from Evil* (Ventura, CA: Regal Books, 2001), 233–234.

John Benefiel, *Breaking the Strongman Over America*

Dr. John Benefiel is an American apostle who leads a network of congregations but has also been involved in spiritual warfare in many parts of the world. He engages in spiritual mapping—the process of outlining the territory of spiritual control and oppression. In this he studies history and archaeology. There are many examples in this book. He has engaged in spiritual warfare with intercessors and leaders in many countries. His work connects to the sins of racism and the oppression and covenant breaking by the government with native Americans. The book deals with extraordinary efforts in Oklahoma in repentance and forgiveness and the great change in unity that has begun.

By far, one of the worst ways that the covenant-breaking spirit manifested was through the Tulsa Race Riot in 1921. Another manifestation occurred early in Oklahoma's history when strife broke out between Tulsa and Oklahoma City. Tulsa's city fathers wanted Tulsa to be the capital of the state of Sequoia while Oklahoma City would be in a different state, Oklahoma. The federal government refused to bow to their wishes, and both cities were located in Oklahoma.

It is my understanding that the break point between the two proposed states was roughly around I-35. When I first came to Oklahoma, you could drive on Turner Turnpike, between the two cities, and feel the warfare Then another political war broke out because Tulsa wanted to be the capital. We still war against that spirit of pride today. We have bathed the Turner Turnpike in prayer as we've driven that route so many times over the years. At one point...[we] vowed together over Communion that we would marry the two cities and see them reside together in unity.

Another way that covenant breaking manifests here is in a lack of unity. One of the pastors told me that he had been part of every single pastor's group that had risen up in Tulsa for 18 years, and not one of them stayed together. Although Tulsa is blessed with some of the greatest ministries in the world, because of the taproot of pride and covenant breaking, gaining ground in unity has been very difficult....

I believe that we are further ahead than other states because we've focused on covenant. It's a lot like marriage; you can mess up and make a lot of mistakes, but if you focus on covenant it will work out....

Dealing with these issues in prayer and repentance then brought great change.

John Benefiel, *Binding the Strongman Over America* (Oklahoma City, OK: Benefiel Ministries, 2012), 134, 140.

Chapter 9

ANGELS, DEMONS, AND SPIRITUAL WARFARE IN THE REVELATION

THE BOOK OF Revelation presents a more concentrated presentation of spiritual warfare, with angels and demonic powers, than can be found in any other biblical book. Yet, it is profoundly difficult to draw out literal meaning. The book is highly symbolic, and literal implications are debated with great fervor. I have sought to provide my own understanding in my book *Passover, the Key to the Book of Revelation*. In this book I argue that the context for interpretation of the Book of Revelation is the Passover/Exodus. This includes the elements of plagues as God's judgments, the announcement of plagues by prophets like Moses and Elijah (Revelation 11), an Antichrist figure like Pharaoh, and the defeat of the armies that oppose God.

John has a marvelous revelation of Jesus in chapter 1. He is told that the seven stars in the right hand of Yeshua in the vision were the angels of the seven churches of Asia Minor, present-day Turkey. The letters are addressed to the angel of each church. Does this mean that the angel is to deliver the message to each church, or is the angel the head elder of the church of the city and he is to receive the message and deliver it to his church? Interpreters are divided. I believe it is best to see the angels here as the leaders of their respective churches who are to deliver God's message, since John is to convey these messages.

In Revelation 4, John is called up to heaven and sees the throne of God reminiscent of the vision of Isaiah 6 and Ezekiel 1. The twenty-four elders are probably human figures and may represent the churches or those who have died, or the twelve patriarchs and the twelve apostles who figure so prominently in the description of the New Jerusalem in Revelation 21. The four living creatures of the vision in the Hebrew Bible are again depicted. They are angelic figures. The four living creatures (angels) give glory, honor, and praise to Him who sits on the throne. The twenty-four elders respond to this and fall down worship Him who lives forever.

In chapter 5, John describes a mighty angel who is part of the vision. A scroll is in the right hand of the one who sits on the throne and the angel proclaims, "Who is worthy to break the seals and open the scroll?" (v. 2). The Lamb, Yeshua, is the only one who can take the scroll and open it. After this we read that the four living creatures and the twenty-four elders fell down before the Lamb. The text then speaks of the twenty-four elders, each one with a harp and holding golden bowls full of incense, which are the prayers of the saints. The prayers of the saints come up to heaven and are depicted as incense in these bowls. So one can see the literal aspect at least in the sense that the prayers of the saints are conveyed in heaven and are very special.

Verses 11–12 speaks of thousands upon thousands of angels, ten thousand times ten thousand, encircling the throne and singing, "Worthy is the Lamb..."

The Lamb opens the seals in chapter 6, which depict God's judgments in symbols. First was a white horse with a rider with a bow wearing a crown and conquering. Next is a red horse with a rider given power to take peace from the earth. Then a black horse and its rider holding a pair of scales in his hand are portrayed. The scales are for weighing produce and the prices indicating there is scarcity. The fourth seal reveals a pale horse and its rider is named Death, and Hades (the grave) was following him. They had power to kill a fourth of the earth by the sword, famine, plague, and wild beasts.

Are these merely symbolic representations of the judgments of conquering, war, scarcity, and finally death? Or are there really mighty angelic powers under God's authority who carry out His direction and bring about these judgments? It is not necessary to know. However, these judgments have been seen in history and have in some regions killed the kinds of numbers set forth here.

The fifth seal reveals the martyrs for the Gospel who cry out for God's judgment and to avenge their blood. A very important principle of spiritual warfare is then presented. Martyrdom is one of the key means in extending the Kingdom and bringing the judgments of God. There is a number known to God that is the adequate number to complete His work in martyrdom. Martyrdom is not something to be always fought against but something to be embraced when required by the Gospel.

In chapter 7 we have the vision of the 144,000 from the twelve tribes of Israel and also the great multitude from every nation, tribe, people, and language. In this context we read about the angels standing around the throne and the four living creatures and the twenty-four elders, who again fall down on their faces and worship God.

In chapter 8 we read about the seven trumpets that are revealed when the seventh seal is opened. Seven angels who stand before God were given seven trumpets. Another angel was given much incense which he offered with the prayers of the saints on the golden altar before the throne. This is reminiscent of the golden altar of incense, first in the tabernacle and later in the temple. The angel took a censer and filled it with fire from the altar. When he hurled it to the earth there were thunder, rumblings, flashes of lightning, and an earthquake. This leaves us with a question. Are angels really acting from God's assignments to bring judgments to earth? My view is that the Book of Revelation is saying that angels are involved, but the book describes this in a highly symbolic and non-literal way. Therefore when each angel sounds his trumpet, various judgments take place on earth; and these are terrible and severe judgments, but as yet not the worst in the book.

Chapter 9 presents what is in my view the strangest vision in the Book of Revelation. After the fifth angel blows his trumpet, a star fallen from the sky to the earth was given the key to the shaft that leads to the abyss. Usually a star is a ruler in biblical symbolism. Who is this star? Satan? We are not told. Out of the abyss, we read, came great locusts. What are these locusts? They appear to be demonic figures, but they are completely under the sovereignty of God. They were only given permission to harm the people who did not have the seal of God on their foreheads. They were also not given power to kill these people but only to torture them for five months. Satan and his demons are usually depicted as delighting to torture and harm human beings. Does God's allowance and satanic desire come into sync at this point? This is a very hard text. In addition, the description of the locusts shows that they are not locusts at all but supernatural beings with something resembling crowns of gold on their heads with faces like human beings, hair like a woman's hair, and teeth like lions' teeth. They had wings, and the sound of their wings together was like the thundering of many horses and chariots. They had tails and were able to sting people with the tails and the agony was like the sting of a scorpion. Their king was the angel of the abyss whose name is Abaddon or Apollyon, which means destruction. Involvement with evil does bring a terrible sting, at least eventually; and like a woman's hair, evil can attract. However, in all my readings I have never read a fully coherent interpretation of what literal meaning can be taken from this text other than to say it appears that demonic hosts under the ultimate sovereignty of God both mislead and torture human beings.

When the sixth angel blew his trumpet, we read of four angels bound at the Euphrates River. These four now are released to kill a third of mankind. There is also a vision of two hundred million troops. Are these demonic troops? They ride horses out of whose mouths issue fire and smoke and sulfur. A third of mankind was killed by the plagues that came from these horses. The idea that this is the Chinese army, as in some dispensational interpretations, simply does not fit the symbolism that is not of a literal human army.

Chapter 10 opens again with a mighty angel from heaven. He is described as,

> ...robed in a cloud, with a rainbow above his head; his face was like the sun, and his legs like fiery pillars. He was holding a little scroll, which lay open in his hand. He planted his right foot on the sea and his left foot on the land, and he gave a loud shout like the roar of a lion. When he shouted the voices of the seven thunders spoke.
>
> —REVELATION 10:1–3

John is told to not write what the seven thunders said. It is interesting that this angel is described in terms used to describe Yeshua in chapter 1. However, this is not Yeshua, but a mighty angel. It must have been seen as a huge figure in his placing one foot on the land and one on the sea. The seven thunders are also either a non-person personification or other angelic figures whose voices sounded like thunder. This angel swears that there will be no more delay, but that in the day of the sounding of the seventh trumpet, the mystery of God will be accomplished. I think the best interpretation of this mystery is the completion of those who will compose the body of Messiah. This angel takes the little scroll and gives it to John to eat. It is as sweet as honey in his mouth but bitter or sour in his stomach.

In chapter 11 the seventh angel blows his trumpet, and this announces the Kingdom of God triumphing over all the earth and the whole earth becoming submitted to the reign of the Messiah.

The seals, trumpets, and bowls of wrath provide us with a linear progression of events in the Book of Revelation. However, there are many passages that are excursuses and transcend the linear progress. Chapter 12 is one of those passages. This chapter depicts a woman who is clothed with the sun and with the moon under her feet and with twelve stars on her head. I believe this is the nation of Israel though, of course, the Israelite who gave birth was Miriam. Then John sees an enormous red dragon. This dragon had seven heads, ten horns, and seven crowns on this head. This could indicate kings that are controlled by the dragon with the horns as the strength of these kings. The dragon is a symbolic depiction of Satan, the devil. That his tail swept a third of the stars out of the sky would fit the contemporary Jewish idea that a third of the angels fell through the influence of Satan, a former archangel. The dragon tried to devour the Child when He was born. This was the case with Herod's attempt to kill the newly born King Jesus. That the Child was snatched up to heaven is probably a reference to the ascension of Jesus after His resurrection. The woman has to flee but will be protected in the last tribulation, which is described as approximately three and one-half years.

Spiritual warfare is portrayed at its height. Michael and his angels fought against the dragon and his angels. The dragon and his angels were not strong enough and lost their place in heaven. The dragon was hurled down to earth with his angels, and here he is named as the devil or Satan who leads the whole world astray. This hurling down is followed by a loud voice in heaven speaking, beginning with the word "now." The salvation and power of the Kingdom of God has come. Satan is said to be the one who is "the accuser of our brothers and sisters, who accuses them before our God day and night" (v. 10).

We are left with many mysteries. When was Satan and his angels hurled down? Was it in pre-history before Adam was created? Or was it subsequent to the Book of Job where Satan is pictured in heaven having access to God? Or was it through the ministry of Yeshua's followers where Yeshua announced in Luke 10 that He saw Satan fall from heaven? Or is falling from heaven whenever the devil loses his power over a territory due to the progress of the Gospel? We are not given a clear answer, though most Christians have been taught a clear progression and think that Satan and his angels were cast out shortly after his fall. A later casting down is then interpreted as from the air but not heaven where God dwells. However, with regard to literal answers to these questions, we really do not know. Verse

12 states that the heavens are to rejoice because Satan has been cast down, but a woe is pronounced to the earth and sea because the devil is now on earth and filled with fury because he knows his time is short.

Revelation 12:11 teaches one of the most important keys to spiritual warfare: "They triumphed over him by the blood of the Lamb and by the word of their testimony; and they did not love their lives so much as to shrink from death."

The meaning of this is that we overcome the devil when we stand on the basis of our position in covenant, a covenant based in the blood of the Lamb. This testimony is also strengthened by the willingness to die for our faith. I would add as taught earlier in this book that the Lord's Supper is a great part of this testimony where we show the Lord's death and nullify the power of the whole demonic reality that seeks to attack God's people.

The dragon now pursues the woman, but she is preserved in the desert. This well fits the desert of Jewish history but also the preservation of the Jewish people. When the dragon cannot destroy her, he makes war on the rest of her offspring. That offspring is the people from all nations and tribes rendered in Revelation 7. These people are said to obey God's commandments and hold to the testimony of Yeshua.

Revelation 13 presents another picture of last days spiritual warfare. It presents a beast that comes out of the sea (peoples). Again there are seven heads, ten crowns, and a blasphemous name on each head. The beast is an image generally interpreted to be the final antichrist, a very credible interpretation. He is in the image of the emperor of Rome, probably Nero, who by this time was already dead. The dragon, already identified as the devil, gave the beast his throne, power, and authority. The beast makes war on the saints and conquers them. We later find that this conquering is not so complete as the verse would seem to indicate since later chapters will show that this conquering is partial. The inhabitants of the earth worship the beast.

Then in verse 11 there is a description of another beast who had two horns. He exercised all the authority of the first beast. He seems to be a prophetic figure in support of the first beast. He is able to do miraculous signs, including bringing fire from heaven in full view of men. He deceives the inhabitants of the earth and charges them to make an image (idol) of the first beast. The idol acts almost like a modern robot! He appears to have been given breath and was able to cause (through orders?) all who refused to worship the image to die. He also forced everyone to receive a mark on their hand or forehead as a requirement for buying and selling. The number of the beast is 666. The letters for Nero seem to be the best interpretation; so we are looking for an evil figure like Nero.

Revelation 14:6–12 presents us with three angels that make announcements. The first is flying in midair with the eternal Gospel to proclaim to every nation, tribe, language, and people. This Gospel, of course, has to be proclaimed and spread by human beings. The angel calls for people to "fear God and give him glory, because the hour of his judgment has come. Worship him who made the heavens, the earth, the sea and the springs of water" (v. 7).

This makes it obvious that the conquering by the beast is not total, for in this time of tribulation the Gospel still goes forth. Indeed, the second angel follows and proclaims, "Fallen! Fallen is Babylon the Great, which made all the nations drink the maddening wine of her adulteries" (v. 8).

The third angel followed them and announces that those who worship and follow the beast and his image will "drink the wine of God's fury, which has been poured full strength into the cup of his wrath" (v. 10). They will be tormented in the presence of the angels and the Lamb.

Angels are here represented as announcing those things that will happen on earth, but of course, a person on earth will, I believe, be announcing what the angel announces, in this case John.

Chapter 14:14–20 presents two figures. The first is on a white cloud and is spoken of as "one like a son of man with a crown of gold on his and a sharp sickle in his hand" (v. 14). (The reference is possibly Daniel 7—the son of man passage.) Another angel comes out of the temple in heaven and calls to him and tells him, "Take your sickle and reap, because the time to reap has come, for the harvest of the earth ripe" (v. 15). He then harvests the earth.

Another angel came out of the temple who himself had a sharp sickle plus another angel who had charge of fire. He calls to the angel with the sharp sickle and says he is to take his sickle and gather the grapes from the earth's vine. This angel gathered the grapes and threw them into the great winepress of God's wrath.

There are two harvests described with two different figures doing the harvesting. It seems that the first is the harvest of salvation. The second is the harvest of wrath. This fits the teaching of Yeshua with regard to the last harvest of wheat and tares or the sorting of the fish at the end of the age. Many interpreters believe the first figure is Jesus, not just an angel.

It seems that this is where the Book of Revelation places the rapture of the saints, near the end of the tribulation but before the bowls of wrath.

Chapter 15 presents seven angels with seven last plagues. The text speaks of those who had been victorious over the beast and his image. The seven angels are described as dressed in "clean, shining linen and wore golden sashes around their chests" (v. 6).

One of the four living creatures gives a bowl to each angel. The bowls are filled with God's wrath. Thus we have the symbolism of a bowl poured out as a prophetic angelic act that leads to the judgments described in chapter 16.

After the sixth angel pours out the contents of his bowl, we read that "three impure spirits that looked like frogs…came out of the mouth of the dragon, out of the mouth of the beast and out of the mouth of the false prophet" (16:13). We are told they are the spirits of demons performing miraculous signs and "they go out to the kings of the whole world to gather them for battle on the great day of God Almighty" (v. 14).

I have often wondered at the incredible foolishness of those who engage in the final battle against the returning Lamb, the Lord Yeshua. Here we see that there are great false signs and wonders that draw them into battle.

Chapter 17 provides us with a picture of Jezebel, the whole system of Babylon. An angel carries John away in the Spirit to see the image of Jezebel as a woman riding on a scarlet beast. The angel interprets the symbols of the beast and does associate the seven heads with Rome (seven hills) and seven kings.

Chapter 18 opens with another angel coming down from heaven with great authority and splendor and announcing the fall of Babylon the great, a symbol of both Rome and the last days final empire that opposes the Kingdom of God.

In Chapter 19 a mighty angel tells John to write, "Blessed are those who are invited to the wedding supper of the Lamb" (v. 9).

John was so awed that he fell at his feet to worship him, but is told,

> See that you do not do that! I am your fellow servant, and of your brethren who have the testimony of Jesus. Worship God! For the testimony of Jesus is the spirit of prophecy.
>
> —REVELATION 19:10, NKJV

Note that John worships Yeshua as deity with no correction but the mighty angel is clearly distinguished as one that is not to be worshiped. The worship of angels was sometimes a heretical practice opposed by the apostles.

In verses 17 through 20 we read of an angel standing in the sun that cries out with a loud voice to the birds to come to a great feast due to the coming slaughter of the armies that will gather to fight the Lamb of God. The beast and the false prophet were thrown alive into the lake of fire.

Chapter 20 first speaks about the thousand years, the millennium, and the destiny of the dragon, the ancient serpent, the devil, or Satan. Here all the designations are used. An angel having the key to the abyss with a great chain, throws him into the abyss. It is locked and sealed so that he cannot deceive the nations for a thousand years. Premillennialists believe that there will thus be a thousand years of world peace under the rule of Yeshua before one more temptation of the nations at the end of this. Others see the limitation of the devil during this age due to the work of the Church and that the Church age is the Millennium. The whole thrust of the Book of Revelation does not seem to fit this.

In verses 7 through 10 we read about the end of Satan. After the thousand years are over, he is released from his prison to again deceive the nations. There is one more gathering for battle. They surrounded the camp of God's people (Israel?), but fire from heaven devoured them. There is no long process as described in the early battles of the Book of Revelation. Then we read that the devil was "thrown into the lake of burning sulfur, where the beast and the false prophet had been thrown. They will be tormented day and night for ever and ever" (v. 10).

Not much needs to be said in interpretation except to just say that the devil finally receives a terrible end. This end will be shared by others, for we read, "Anyone whose name was not found written in the book of life was thrown into the lake of fire" (v. 15).

Again in chapter 21, verses 9 and 10, John has an angelic guide who says to him,

> Come, I will show you the bride, the wife of the Lamb. And he carried me away in the Spirit to a mountain great and high, and showed me the Holy City, Jerusalem, coming down out of heaven from God.

The angel had a measuring rod and measured the city. It was 1,400 miles square and 1,400 miles high. The height may not be a cube, but ascending levels in a pyramid shape.

In chapter 22:1, the angel showed John the river of life that came from the throne of God. Then in verse 6 there is an affirmation of the place of angels in revelation.

> The angel said to me, "These words are trustworthy and true. The Lord, the God of the prophets, sent his angel to show his servants the things that must soon take place.

Then there is finally one more exhortation to not worship the angel that gives the revelation.

> I, John, am the one who heard and saw these things. And when I had heard and seen them, I fell down to worship at the feet of the angel who had been showing them to me. But he said to me, "Don't do that! I am a fellow servant with you and with your brothers the prophets and with all who keep the words of this scroll. Worship God!"
>
> —REVELATION 22:8–9

Then the angel concludes with these words,

> Do not seal up the words of the prophecy of this scroll, because he time is near. Let the one who does wrong continue to do wrong; let the vile person continue to be vile; let the one who does right continue to do right; and the holy person continue to be holy.
>
> —REVELATION 22:10–11

In conclusion, the Book of Revelation shows the most intense level of spiritual warfare. It shows angels, demons, the Devil, the Antichrist, the false prophet, and amazing upheavals on earth due to this warfare. The weapons are prayer, testimony, standing on the ground of Yeshua's covenant blood, and embracing a radical commitment that is willing to die for the faith. This orientation will gain the ultimate victory.

EXCURSUS

Eddie Hennen and Michael L. Smith, *Strategic Prayer*
In this manual on strategic prayer, the authors give much information on researching a situation, a territory, etc., and developing strategic prayer. They also warn about launching out and addressing the princes of darkness over a territory. Prayer has to be led by the Spirit and prophetic led by those who have real authority and such addressing of the powers is exceptional. Here is one story from their book.

> Eddie and I helped start a church in the fall of 1982 in Houston, Texas. While researching Houston, we uncovered some strategic historical information about how territorial spirits had gained the legal right to our city. So in the winter of 1983, I was praying for Houston, and day after day I asked the Lord to show me the territorial spirits over it. Finally, with an air of confidence, after about six weeks, I felt God had given me the names of the principalities of Houston. Zealously, I began to attack and blast through warfare prayer by saying, "You spirit of death, get out of my city. We don't want you here. I stand against your every scheme to steal, kill, and destroy."
>
> After several weeks of attacking the devil, I came dangerously close to death. I developed an infection from a gall bladder attack and came within twelve hours of dying from peritonitis of the spleen and liver. Within fourteen months, I had almost destroyed my family. Eddie and I had six surgeries, three of them not covered by insurance. We had depleted $35,000 in savings and were on the brink of losing our home. With a growing family, a new

baby, and an eighteen-month-old church that had just lost its first senior pastor, I was close to "giving up in the road." The church was struggling, we were struggling, and the enemy was laughing. I was experiencing what some call "the dark night of the soul."

After our situation settled, about fifteen months later, I asked the Lord about this. He spoke into my heart clear. *Alice, I told you the names of the spirits over Houston, but you didn't ask me what to do with the revelation.* I couldn't believe it! Now I know. We have authority to deal with the enemy, but our authority is ambassadorial. The Lord's time and instruction are absolutely crucial in the fight. I was fighting the battle on my own without His direction. I learned that just because we have a diagnosis doesn't mean God has given us an assignment. I responded to this, and it was a costly lesson to learn.

Excerpt taken from *Strategic Prayer* by Eddie Smith, copyright © 2007. Used by permission of author.

Rolland and Heidi Baker, *Always Enough*

In one of the greatest stories of a great move of God in a nation, *Always Enough* tells the story of the work of Rolland and Heidi Baker in Mozambique, Africa. Thousands of orphans have been changed and thousands of churches planted. The signs and wonders level in this ministry has been amazing. This is an excerpt from a time of warfare during a cholera epidemic that began in the Baker's center.

Challenges to our faith in Jesus did not stop. Even as we received daily reports of desperation from the flooded north, a terrible outbreak of cholera hit our center at Zimpeto near the capital city of Maputo....Within days we had taken seventy children, pastors and workers to a special cholera hospital in town. This was actually a big tent, strictly quarantined, filled with "cholera tables," bare wood beds with holes in them and buckets underneath for nonstop diarrhea and vomiting. Every patient was in an IV drip.

Many had died in this emergency hospital. Maputo's health officials were terrified of a city-wide epidemic. Maputo's director of health put her finger in Heidi's face and told her, "You will be responsible for killing half of Maputo!."... Soon city police were involved, intent on shutting down our entire center and ministry....

Only Heidi was allowed to visit the tent hospital. Every day she would go in and spend hours and hours with our kids, holding them, soaking them in prayer, declaring that they would live and not die. They vomited on her, covered her with filth and slowly grew weaker. Many were on the edge of death, their eyes sunken and rolling back. The doctors were shocked by hear lack of concern for herself and were certain she would die along with many of our children.

Our stress level was the highest ever....Twenty of our pastors from the north were also in the tent and dying. Some of our weaker pastors desperately wanted to go home, certain that they would all die if they stayed with us. Heidi and I were ready yet again to quit if God did not do something.

But during all this the Holy Spirit kept falling on our meetings. Again and again all visitors would come to Jesus and hungrily drink in His presence. A strong spirit of intercession came over your stronger pastors, who would pray all hours, not only for our cholera victims, but for the suffering of the whole nation. Intercessory prayer groups in the U.S. and Canada and around the world began to pray intensely for us.

Our entire future in Mozambique was in question. No one had any more answers. Our weakness was complete. Then some of the children began coming home from the hospital even as others were being taken there. And then there were no new cases. Extraordinary. And then everyone was home. Just like that, the cholera was gone, and Heidi was fine.

The doctors and nurses at the hospital were in a state of shock and wonder. The director of health again put a finer in Heidi's face: "You! This is God! The only reason you got through this was God! You and dozens of these children should be dead!" Eight of the medical staff there wanted to work with us immediately. "This is miraculous! You know God! We've never seen God do anything like this. We've never seen such love! We don't want to work here anymore. We want to work with you!"

We did not lose a single person who lived with us at Zimpeto.

So in a matter of days our worst crisis turned into a wave of peace and joy at our center.

Excerpt from *Always Enough* by Rolland and Heidi Baker, copyright © 2003. Used by permission of Chosen, a division of Baker Publishing Group.

CONCLUSIONS ON ANGELS, DEMONS, AND SPIRITUAL WARFARE

WE HAVE NOW thoroughly searched the Bible on the themes of angels, demons, and spiritual warfare. What have we found?

First, there is a unified teaching in the whole Bible that, besides human beings, there are super human spirits called angels and evil spirits called demons. The earlier writings of the Hebrew Bible are very sketchy with regard to these spirits. Angels are represented as messengers of God and those who enforce God's decrees. We see this in the very beginning in Genesis 3 with the cherubim angel that guards the way back to the Garden of Eden. However, there are few angelic appearances in the earliest texts of the Bible and some of these angelic appearances may be the pre-incarnate Messiah. In Genesis 18 we have the Messiah/God figure who speaks with Abraham and two other angels that visit Sodom and Gomorrah and take Lot and his daughters from the city, protecting them from their totally perverted neighbors.

ANGELS

The name LORD of hosts is an indication that God has angelic armies. We see such armies in the stories of Elijah and Elisha. The Psalms speak about angelic figures. Psalm 8 notes the creation of human beings, perhaps lower than angelic figures, depending on the translation, but destined to be higher than the angels. Angels are represented in the tabernacle, the temple, and as guarding the ark and in the great visions of Isaiah (chapter 6) and in Ezekiel (chapter 1). In Daniel we are given more information with regard to angels that bring answers to prayer. We read that the angel Gabriel was resisted by the prince of Persia but that Michael the archangel came and helped him to bring a message in answer to Daniel's prayer. So we can say that in the Hebrew Bible there is not a lot of information about angels but angels are clearly understood to exist to interact as messengers and as those enforcing God's decrees. The Hebrew Bible, in its lack of emphasis, seems to discourage an overemphasis on angels.

The roles of angels in the New Testament Scriptures are not different, but the angelic realm is more revealed. The angel Gabriel announces the conception of Yeshua to Miriam (Mary) and also reveals himself to Zechariah and announces the conception of John. Angels minister to Yeshua, strengthening and comforting him. An angel helps the apostles escape from prison and later an angel in an amazing way leads Peter to escape. The angel can open locks, release from chains, and lead through passageways! Angels are so very real in these accounts. Angels continue their role throughout the New Testament; and in the final book, The Revelation, angels are the guides of John, are revealed in places in heaven, and finally shown as those who blow trumpets, empty bowls of God's wrath, and announce great judgments. There is no record of calling out to angels, praying to angels, or otherwise having a religious ceremonial connection to angels. They simply are at the behest of God when we pray to God and are sometimes sent when we are in need of aid. Angels are simply supernatural beings that do God's bidding to further His purposes in the world and aid believers. Some are mightier than others; such as in the case of Michael, called an archangel, meaning charge over other angels. There very probably are other archangels.

DEMONS

Conclusions about demons are more difficult to draw. We use the term *demons* for supernatural conscious beings of evil at all levels of power and authority. Demonic power, at least by later biblical interpretation, begins in Genesis 3 with the serpent and the temptation of Adam and Eve. He is identified as Satan and not just a lesser demon. As we progress in the biblical accounts we confront demonic power, though not by name, in the accounts of Joseph and the magicians of Egypt and in the account of Moses who confronts the Egyptian magicians. The commandments against idolatry are at the center of dealing with the demonic power as well as commands against all occult involvement, from divination to mediums and calling on the dead. We are not explicitly told that the issue is demonic power behind idolatry and behind occult practices. This is made clear in the New Covenant Scriptures.

In the New Testament we encounter demons first of all as oppressing individuals. The right term is not possessed by but demonized. Yeshua casts out demons. Casting out demons is a sign of the Kingdom. Yeshua does this with unique authority and it is characteristic of His ministry. We find in the discussion on His deliverance ministry that Satan has power and authority over demonic hosts. (See Matthew 12 and Luke 11.) Satan is the one who is said to have tested Yeshua in the wilderness after His baptism. We already see in the Gospels the idea that he leads a kingdom that influences human societies for evil. However, in the spread of the Gospel though the seventy, Yeshua sees Satan fall like lightening. (See Luke 10.)

The Book of Acts continues to show the same patterns. There is deliverance. We see false prophecy through evil spirits. It is in the Epistles that we find a larger description of a hierarchy of evil, of princes of darkness (principalities and powers) that Paul says he tears down or brings down. The texts that speak about these things speak in terms of presenting truth that has an effect. The "wiles of the devil" is described in Ephesians 6, for which we must have the whole armor of God. The devil tempts and tests believers, but we are to resist him. The general Epistles emphasize this. The Book of Revelation shows a hierarchy of evil powers working through people, and ultimately through an Antichrist and a false prophet. All these evil ones are defeated in the end and all ultimately end up in the lake of fire. It is important to note that the Bible does not give clear answers as to the identity of demons. They are connected to fallen angels and may in many cases be fallen angels, or they could be other kinds of evil spirits that are under the direction of fallen angels that are lesser. We are simply not told.

Spiritual Warfare

Finally, we summarize the biblical content on spiritual warfare. In the Hebrew Bible spiritual warfare was connected to moral and ritual holiness; the latter was symbolic. In this regard, the center of warfare was in maintaining the tabernacle and later the temple system for the forgiveness of sin and for purification. In addition, it was to keep free from all idolatry and occult practice. Spiritual warfare in the Hebrew Bible includes real physical warfare; and through destroying the Canaanites who were seen as totally corrupt, we could say a demonic society is destroyed. Eliminating the Canaanites and all idolatry was crucial if Israel was to be a light to the nations. Revivals in Israel's history were connected to destroying all idols and fleeing all occult practices. We do not see a deliverance ministry. The Bible does look toward the defeat of the powers of evil, spoken of in Isaiah 27 as the destruction of Leviathan, the scheming serpent that dwells in the midst of the sea (the peoples of the earth). Daniel's fasting and prayer have effect in bringing the fulfillment of Israel's return of the land after seventy years of captivity; but the answer was hindered by an evil prince of darkness, called the prince of Persia, who hindered the arrival of Gabriel. So the book portrays a battle or some kind of resistance in the heavens and not only on earth. There are no instructions on defeating these powers other than prayer and obedience.

The New Testament instruction on spiritual warfare is much richer. The ministry of Yeshua is largely spiritual warfare. The preaching of the Gospel with signs and wonders delivers people from poverty, grief, and frustration. The deliverance ministry confronts the powers of darkness directly. We find that some or many ailments are demonic based. The solution is a power confrontation by the anointed minister. This ability is passed to the twelve in Luke 9 and then to the seventy. There is no reason why deliverance ministry should not be seen as a key in spiritual warfare today.

Most of the emphasis on spiritual warfare in the New Testament consists first of all in prayer by which we abide in the vine, Yeshua. Then we are to read, meditate on, and know the Word so that we are able to abide in His power and anointing and to quote the Word in resisting the devil or demonic powers. Fasting is another exercise to increase the presence and power of God and to be more effective in confronting the powers of darkness in deliverance ministry. Demons are addressed in this ministry. In addition, Timothy is exhorted to see that there is prayer for civil authorities that Jesus believers might live a life of peace and be free to spread the Gospel. It appears as well that taking communion, the Lord's Supper, in unity shows the power of Yeshua's death. Showing this, I believe, has an effect on the powers of darkness that were stripped of their power when Yeshua died on the cross. We are told to resist the devil simply by living a godly life and being on guard and asking the presence and power of the Spirit for discernment and power to do right. This is the emphasis of the general Epistles that portray Satan, the demonic realm, as ready to devour.

The one text that is used for engaging in spiritual warfare by directly addressing the princes of darkness over territories does not seem to be speaking about such activity. Rather, when Paul describes how he defeats the strongholds in people, groups, etc., he speaks of tearing down arguments and presenting the truth with supernatural power. (See 2 Corinthians 10:4.) When Paul says that the weapons of our warfare are not carnal, there is nothing in the text to indicate something more than preaching the Gospel with power and signs following, doing healing and deliverance ministry to individuals, praying (which is a mighty weapon), and refuting false teaching and arguments with anointed power. Others have noted worship as a weapon of warfare, and that is probably true, since we are told in Ephesians 5:18 that singing hymns and spiritual songs is a key to maintaining the power of the Spirit in our lives.

About twenty-four years ago, from the writing of this chapter, there was a great debate in the charismatic world (including the third wave of John Wimber's Vineyard). Wimber came out with strong criticisms of those movements in prayer which spoke about territorial spirits and would address such princes of darkness after discerning the nature of these spirits. They would sometimes be addressed in the form of commands that demanded them to be bound and to loose the territory or the people of the region from their power. For example: "I come against the prince of mammon over this city and command you to be bound and to loose this city from your power." It was almost like deliverance ministry applied to regions of the world, cities, counties, and sometimes whole countries. Sometimes I attended prayer meetings with loud tongues of intercession and where people would shout out commands to the demonic powers over their city, region or nation. "We command you to… "

For Wimber, it seemed that sometimes these folks were simply beating the air. But at other times, Wimber believed they touched real high up demonic power without sufficient authority to do so and were therefore in great danger. Wimber believed that some lost their lives doing this. In the early 90s I wrote an article on this for Mike Bickle. My view was as follows and remains the same to this day.

There is nothing in the Bible that teaches us to address the princes of darkness directly to command them to be bound and to loose the people in a territory from their power.

However, it would seem reasonable that prophets could discern that such powers were exercising authority through people in a territory. It would also be reasonable to pray and fast for a breakthrough in the Gospel and to ask God to rebuke these powers and to nullify their power.

However, I do not believe that Bible precludes a prophetic word coming upon someone who is a truly credible and proven prophet who would address and command a demonic prince of darkness over a territory. Otherwise prophecy would be circumscribed in a way that the Bible does not preclude. However, if this is to be done, it would have to come through a truly anointed proven prophetic person who knows what he is doing, and if over a territory, should be supported by the unity of the leaders of the church in the area where the princes of darkness are addressed. Division empowers the demonic realm, whereas true unity in Yeshua undercuts demonic power. I would think that such action, to address and command higher up spirits in this way, should be exceptional and that it is generally better to ask God and to pray and fast for the powers of darkness to be nullified.

ABOUT THE AUTHOR

D R. DANIEL JUSTER received his BA from Wheaton College, his MDiv from McCormick Theological Seminary, did two years in the philosophy of religion program of Trinity Evangelical Divinity School, and received his ThD from New Covenant International Seminary. Dr. Juster has been involved in the Messianic Jewish movement since 1972. He was the founding president and general secretary of the Union of Messianic Jewish Congregations for nine years; the senior leader of Beth Messiah Congregation, Rockville, Maryland, for twenty-two years; and presently is a member of the apostolic team that governs Tikkun International Ministries. Tikkun International is an umbrella organization for an apostolic network of leaders, congregations, and ministries who share a common commitment—namely the restoration of Israel and the Church. Dr. Juster is also the director of the Tikkun America of congregations; and as such, he provides oversight to some twenty congregations in the USA. He presently ministers personally under the name of Restoration from Zion, a Tikkun ministry.

Tikkun is committed to: (1) training; (2) sending out and supporting congregational planters in the USA, Israel, and other countries; (3) fostering Jewish ministry in local churches; and (4) helping to support an international network of Bible and graduate schools for training leaders for the Jewish vineyard and for work in the rest of the Church (presently there are schools in Odessa, Moscow; Buenos Aires, Argentina; and Zimbabwe).

Dr. Juster has authored several books, including *Jewish Roots: A Foundation of Biblical Theology*; *Dynamics of Spiritual Deception*; *Jewishness and Jesus*; *The Biblical World View: An Apologetic*; *Relational Leadership*; *The Irrevocable Calling*; *One People, Many Tribes*; and *Mutual Blessing*. He has been a featured speaker at many conferences, both nationally and internationally.

Presently, Dan and his wife, Patty, spend most of their year in Israel near Jerusalem and four months' travel in the United States. He has three married children and nine grandchildren who live in the Israel.

CONTACT THE AUTHOR

Email: danieljuster@gmail.com